DERBY TRAINMAN
1990-94

Tim Helme

Published by

Top Link Press
toplink@btinternet.com

For my Parents

We shall not cease from exploration,
And the end of all our exploring
Will be to arrive where we started
And know the place for the first time.
T.S. Eliot.

Acknowledgements

I would like to express my gratitude to several people, without whom this book would have been extremely difficult to complete: Richard King, for his recollections, photographs and technical assistance; Philip Helme, also for his recollections and photographs, Jim Riley for his excellent photography of the Denby Branch during 1992, Chris Nutty for the final photograph, and Kim Durose for putting it all together! I would also like to thank the numerous people who read, commented, and offered advice on the draft chapters.

Front Cover – clockwise:
Derby 4 Shed, Mar 1992. Photo: Author.
Official B.R. shed designation badge.
Author on the Denby Branch, Mar 1992. Photo: J. Riley.
Denby North bites the dust, Mar 1992. Photo: Author.
Approaching Holbrook, Jan 1992. Photo: J. Riley.

Back Cover:
Author at Denby North, Jan 1992. Photo: J. Riley.

Contents

Foreword

The grade of Trainman was created during the train crew reorganisation of British Rail in 1988 and was an amalgamation of the traditional grades of Guard and Secondman. Around this time a shortage of drivers was foreseen at Derby due to a number of "old hands" approaching retirement age, so to cover this shortfall, several new recruits were employed straight "off the street." In order for them to gain experience in this very different, almost Victorian, working environment (of which many steam age practices remained), they were employed in the new grade of Trainman. Those who successfully passed the driver selection course at Manchester were designated Trainman (D). On completion of an eight week course, the new Trainmen were then let loose upon the railway network covering, as will be seen, a wide variety of jobs on routes emanating from the Derby area.

Derby train crew were based in the remaining buildings of the old Number 4 Shed, of which only the mess room, locker room and various administration offices still stood. During its prime, 4 Shed housed two turntables and was the running shed of the Derby Loco Works complex. By 1990, its status had been vastly reduced, but a range of motive power could still be found stabled there, with classes 08, 20, 31, 37, as well as the ubiquitous class 47, together with HSTs, Sprinters and first generation DMUs, parked in the adjoining Etches Park Carriage Sidings.

Being versatile (able to work both passenger and freight trains), and also having the Carriage & Wagon Works, Railway Technical Centre, Economic Oil Terminal and Chaddesden Sidings all within close proximity to the depot, no two days were the same for a trainman! But with experience quickly gained (sometimes the hard way!), life on the railway eventually became routine. When the need arose, the senior men of the grade were put forward for driver training, thus covering the predicted shortfall. However, on the 14th of July 1992, came the announcement from the then Conservative government, that the railways of Britain were to be privatised. This comfortable and settled existence railway employees had grown accustomed to was about to change. Uncertainty was the topic of mess rooms up and down the network, as the railway was broken up into business sectors and now run to satisfy the demands of accountants, rather than the needs of the customers, be it passenger or freight.

The Derby area came under the banner of InterCity Midland Cross Country, and as a result, the workload became greatly reduced, leaving only the departmental ballast trains, RTC test work and the occasional passenger job for the trainmen. Endless hours of sitting spare in the mess room ensued, while only at weekends was there a buzz of activity, when on Saturday evenings, procession after procession of departmental ballast trains left the nearby Chaddesden Sidings en-route to various worksites around the Midlands. This situation could never last and during early 1994, redundancy was offered, of which there were many takers. For those left, life carried as normal for a few months, until a further announcement came that Derby was to become an all passenger depot, and that all non-passenger work, together with the role of Trainman, would cease.

Tim Helme's account of life as a Derby Trainman gives a fascinating insight into those last few years of British Railways. The jobs, the characters, and the humour are all here as a lasting reminder.

Written by a driver, who successfully progressed via the Trainman (D) route of employment during this period.

Authors Note

I had originally planned to write an article solely on the Denby Branch, but as this work progressed and the information kept coming, I felt it equally important to profile the other major jobs that Derby Trainmen undertook as well. The rail industry has changed enormously since 1994, but to me, it seems to have lost a lot of its heart and soul in the process. In writing this book, I wanted to look back and provide an account of how things used to be done, and what it was like to be part of an organisation (or even family) that stretched the entire length and breadth of the country.

Tim Helme, Derby, 2006.

The "Denby" approaches Coxbench Crossing, (See Chap 10). Photo: P. Helme, circa 1988.

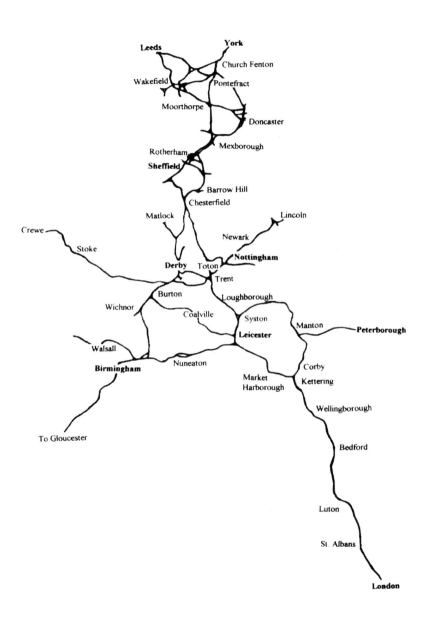

Drawn by Author 2005

Derby Station Area (circa 1990)

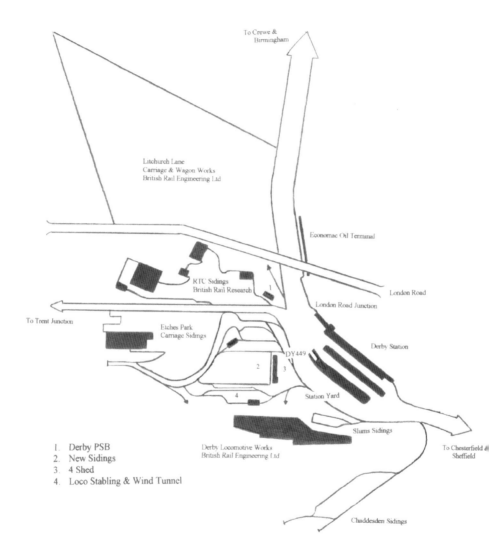

To Crewe &
Birmingham

Litchurch Lane
Carriage & Wagon Works
British Rail Engineering Ltd

Economac Oil Terminal

RTC Sidings
British Rail Research

London Road

London Road Junction

To Trent Junction

Etches Park
Carriage Sidings

Derby Station

DY449

Station Yard

Slums Sidings

1. Derby PSB
2. New Sidings
3. 4 Shed
4. Loco Stabling & Wind Tunnel

Derby Locomotive Works
British Rail Engineering Ltd

To Chesterfield &
Sheffield

Chaddesden Sidings

Drawn by Author 2005

10

1. Mixed Traffic

The process of becoming a Trainman (D) was not an easy one, and becoming a Trainman (D) at my home depot of Derby was especially difficult. For a start, footplate vacancies there were extremely rare, particularly for someone straight off the street. However, towards the end of 1989, fate, or whatever, decreed that I was finally in the right place at the right time, and after my initial application and interview, I was summoned for a formal interview with the Area Train Crew Manager. I have to assume that I met his exacting standards, because not long after, I was dispatched to the Train Crew Selection Centre at Manchester Piccadilly, for some rather intensive testing. After successfully completing all their mechanical, concentration, observation and reaction tests, and a further interview, I was then sent to the railway doctor at Derby for a full medical. After this exhaustive selection process, I was finally offered the position of Trainee Trainman (D) at Derby, but would first have to complete my initial training at Toton depot.

Along with several other new starters, I spent eight weeks in a classroom at Toton learning the fine art of railway operation, as taught by British Rail. The first week was an induction course where we became acquainted with the B.R. Rule Book, as well as the Working Manual (white and pink pages), and the General Appendix. These books became our constant career long companions, as we were required to carry them at all times when on duty. Successful completion of this first week enabled a new starter to undertake the duties of a yard shunter, and a couple of our classmates who'd been employed on this path were dispatched to such locations as Maltby Colliery and Drakelow Power Station to begin their prospective careers. After the induction came the more intensive six week Trainman (G) course, where all the rules and regulations appertaining to the duties and responsibilities of a B.R. guard were mercilessly drummed into us! Provided you passed the rules exam at the end, you officially became a qualified guard…in theory at least! An important section of the Rule Book, and a favourite of any examiner was section M, which dealt with train protection. In the event of an accident or train failure, three detonators, 20 yards apart, had to be placed 300 yards from the train. (Full protection consisted of one at ¼ of a mile, one at ½ a mile, and three at a mile and a ¼) The driver would go forward to protect, whilst the guard or secondman would go back. The brightly coloured detonators contained a small explosive charge and were affixed to the top of the rail by their lead legs. If run over by another train, the resulting detonations would alert that driver to the obstruction ahead. Although there were some in every locomotive cab, train crew also carried ten detonators with them when on duty.

The Rule Book Sections
A   General safety and security responsibilities.
B   Safety when working on or near running lines.
C   Signals.
D   Passing signals at danger, wrong direction working.
H   Working of trains.
J   Shunting.
K   Trains or vehicles detained on running lines or loops.
M   Accidents and failures.
N   Single line working.
R/T   Engineers responsibilities and protection of work
U   Temporary and emergency speed restrictions

Those of us who had successfully completed the testing at Manchester then progressed on to the final week long Trainman (D) course, where we were taught all the duties of the driver's assistant, or secondman. There was another test at the end, this time conducted by the resident traction inspector, but after eight weeks of meticulously ploughing through the Rule Book, I found this one to be relatively straightforward. I was now qualified to act as a guard (pending sufficient road knowledge), and a secondman. All I needed now was some solid practical experience, and Derby didn't disappoint!

Road Learning
The end of the trainman course was by no means the end of the learning process. A Ministry of Transport requirement was for all drivers and guards to have detailed knowledge of the routes they worked over. This knowledge obviously included such things as stations, junctions, signals, gradients, speed limits, shunting movements, etc. Individual routes would be learnt for a set period of time, at the end of which, the senior TCS (Train Crew Supervisor) expected you to sign your road card confirming that you were competent to work a train over said routes. A trainman carrying out the duties of a secondman was exempt from this rule. He could undertake any secondman work as required, since he (supposedly) always accompanied a driver with the necessary knowledge. On the occasional and unavoidable times where a driver or guard was required to operate over a route he didn't sign, a conductor would have to be provided. Conducting train crew obviously had the necessary knowledge and assisted the booked crew over the route. This method of operation also applied to the different types of traction a driver could encounter.

From a trainman's point of view, learning a road was relatively straightforward, but it wasn't enough just to know the names of stations, junctions and nearby settlements between Derby and a certain point. There could be any number of small sidings along the way, or even a major marshalling yard, all with slightly different rules and methods of working, but it was the trainman's job, if he signed the road, to know how to operate in these places…at any time and in any weather! For example, between Derby and Leicester, roughly a distance of 30 miles, there were at least three ballast sidings a Derby trainman would require knowledge of. However, as a certain proportion of our road learning was done from passenger trains, it wasn't always easy to examine these sidings properly. When questioned, most of the drivers you rode with always responded with the famous last words; "That's so and so sidings…don't worry about them, you'll never go in there." So after a week's road learning, you'd happily sign the route, only to find that literally the very next day, you'd be working a job to so and so sidings! You could of course sign the road for passenger work only, but trainmen who made a habit of this quite rightly invited much derision for their colleagues. It was a rather selfish way of always ensuring the secondman position on a weekend ballast job, or avoiding a job completely…particularly if it involved too much work! Another practice, just as unprofessional as work avoidance, was developing a blasé attitude towards road learning. Some people signed roads on a whim, often after travelling over them just once…these were the people who usually slipped up, sometimes endangering others! To be fair, much of the work was common sense and learnt through experience, but I always took road learning seriously, because when you have a freight train waiting to clear the main line at 0200 in the pouring rain, and you're stood at a ground frame (a set of manual point levers) not knowing which lever to pull…then it's too late!

A good example of how seriously I took road learning was when a group of us were sent to learn the main line between Derby and Sheffield. Most of us already signed as far as Ambergate Junction, so travelling backwards and forwards on passenger trains served our needs adequately enough. However, we needed to study Avenue Ground Frame and Sidings, situated near Clay Cross, but instead of hitching a ride on a freight train, I decided we'd stick with the passenger service, alight at Chesterfield Station and walk back! Of course, the distance and journey time between the two points didn't seem too terrible from a coach window travelling at 70 mph, but our little walk turned out to be a six mile round trip on merciless railway ballast! One of my colleagues had just been issued with the latest "Corporate Collection" railway uniform, including new shoes, which were unfortunately giving him a bit of grief. I think he moaned every step of the way, but had occasion to thank me later, as that same year we ended up working a lot of weekend engineering trains on the Erewash Valley Line, many of which required to be run round using Avenue Ground Frame!

When I started at Derby at the beginning of 1990, it was still classed as British Rail London Midland Region, and officially remained so until the 5th of April 1992. As the different business sectors emerged as a prelude to privatisation, management embarked on a period of name changing. As the all-encompassing British Rail name was subtly dispensed with, we were classed in part, as East Midlands (Passenger), before finally being designated as an InterCity (Midland Cross Country) depot. Initially, the different business names or sectors didn't alter the volume of work to pass through Derby. Passenger services were still as important as ever, and the wealth and variety of freight work was most welcome, particularly from a trainman's point of view. To my knowledge, from 1990 right up to eventual privatisation, Derby Trainmen were involved in almost every sphere of operation, except freightliner and automotive trains. We worked coal, petroleum, metals, chemicals, construction, research, departmental, passenger…and even the mail! Even Toton couldn't boast this range of work! Within a couple of years, my road knowledge extended to all points of the compass to accommodate this mixed traffic. I signed as far as Leeds and York in the north, Nottingham and Peterborough in the east, London St. Pancras in the south, Birmingham and Gloucester in the southwest…and no Derby road card was really complete without Crewe in the northwest!

Dangerous Goods

It may have been 1990, but some rules and railway practices hadn't changed much from steam days. Guard's brakevans were still used on trains, but only on two specific types: trains that were unfitted (i.e. without functioning brakes), and trains carrying dangerous goods. However, a noteworthy addition to this rule was our very own Denby job. Brakevans were necessary on this train, simply because of the trainman operated crossings on the branch, (see Chap 10). The three categories of dangerous goods where a brakevan would be required were nuclear flasks, hydrocyanic acid, and toxic gases. The reason for having a brakevan on this kind of work was quite simple, if a problem occurred with the train (e.g. a fire or derailment), the driver would go forward to carry out detonator protection, whilst the guard, who was already at the rear, would go back. This way, no one would have to pass any potentially unstable or damaged wagons…which was rather important considering the nature of the materials being conveyed!

An example of a train conveying dangerous goods, in this case, a nuclear flask. Note the coal hoppers serving as barrier wagons in this particular formation. Photo: P. Helme, 1986.

Derby men weren't normally responsible for any nuclear flask or hydrocyanic acid traffic, but there were at least two toxic gas jobs allocated to us. Unfortunately they both belonged in the senior trainman's link (roster), and it would be nearly two years before I progressed from the junior link to such heady and respected heights! The first job was known as the Bromsgrove tanks, where Derby men worked the train to the sidings at the foot of Blackwell bank (or Lickey incline), southwest of Birmingham. I personally never worked this job, as another depot gained the work before I achieved a place in the top link! However, when I did eventually move up the ladder, I got to work the remaining job many times. This was known as the York tanks, and potential hazards aside, it was one of my favourites (see Chap 9). Much to my exasperation though, the two trainman links were merged not long after!

Unfitted Trains
The reason for having a brakevan on unfitted, or partially fitted trains, was that if a coupling broke and the train became divided, the driver would be able to apply the engine brakes and stop his portion, whilst the guard could do likewise in the brakevan. Unfitted trains were restricted to 25 mph and partially fitted to 35 mph. In the brief period between starting on the railway and BREL (British Rail Engineering Limited) being completely lost forever, the Carriage Works at Litchurch Lane retained a contract with London Underground to refurbish their coaching stock. The job consisted of one complete London Underground train, with a barrier wagon at each end. It was unfitted and therefore required a brakevan. The job originated from the LRT (London Regional Transport) depot at West Ruislip and was worked to the relief cabin at Landor Street Junction by Saltley men…which was exceptionally handy for them, since their depot was situated just around the corner! Whilst the train was making its steady progress up through Buckinghamshire and Northamptonshire, the Derby men would be travelling passenger down to Birmingham New Street, where they would then change for the next local service to Duddeston, the closest station to Saltley. After a short walk through some decidedly dubious streets, the Derby driver and guard would finally reach the depot and make

their presence known to the TCS, before continuing on to the relief cabin. Eventually, the phone in the cabin would ring, informing them that their job was approaching. Once back at Derby, the train would have to be propelled (reversed) under London Road Bridge and into the Carriage Works. Although the place had seen happier days, Litchurch Lane was still a vast site and was rumoured to have 365 sets of hand points…one for each day of the year! It was also a separate signing on the road card, so at this early stage in my career, I needed a conductor into the works…even though I'd just worked the job up from Birmingham, and 4 Shed was less than 100 metres away!

A selection of brakevans at Toton. Photo: R. King.

Other unfitted work that occasionally came our way was the movement of preserved locomotives. These were transported from local preservation societies to the various depot open days around the region. Coalville and Leicester were always popular venues, and it was after one of these events when, along with a driver, I was tasked to return the peaks D1OO *Sherwood Forester*, D8 *Penyghent*, and the green liveried Metrovick to Peak Rail at Matlock. Travelling passenger to Leicester, we made our way across to the depot where our train was waiting. However, my brakevan was missing two vital pieces of equipment. Before departure, I would first have to obtain some coal for the stove, as well as two old-fashioned paraffin side lamps! According to the Rule Book, the brakevan on an unfitted train had to display three red lights on a main line (i.e. a tail light and two side lights), and when on a goods line or loop, a white light must be displayed on the side adjacent to a running line…I was glad I'd paid attention the day they covered this at Toton! These lamps however, were virtually museum pieces and I have no idea where the Leicester TCS obtained a set, but it reinforces what I said earlier about certain practices not changing much from steam days! Fortunately both lamps still had their interchangeable red lenses intact, and their paraffin reservoirs were full, so along with the electric tail light I already had, we were finally ready to depart!

Of course, during the trip from Leicester to Derby, we were switched between the main line and the goods line several times, so I was busy altering lenses for most of the journey! We also generated a bit of interest from the train spotters on Derby Station as we continued northbound…they were no doubt wondering why the guard was leaning out the brakevan fiddling around with two paraffin lamps! At Ambergate Station, the driver obtained the token, which gave us permission to proceed onto the Matlock Branch. I would also need it to operate the ground frame at Matlock Station, which would allow entry into Peak Rail itself. The Matlock Branch is purely a passenger route and I had signed it as such, never really expecting to have to operate the ground frame, or carry out any intensive shunting operations there…some of which would have to take place on private property! It was another one of those instances where I been told not to worry…I'd never have to go in there!

An important thing to remember, which could easily be overlooked in all the excitement, was that the train was unbraked. So before anyone set about uncoupling the engine or brakevan, it was wise to apply at least one handbrake! The owner of the engines at Peak Rail had already witnessed one trainman, who'd forgotten this small point, sprinting after his runaway locos! As soon as we arrived at Matlock, the heavens opened and I got completely soaked in a matter of seconds. By the time I'd figured out the ground frame and finished shunting, I was feeling pretty miserable. Fortunately I'd maintained a nice fire in the brakevan, and hung my clothes to dry as best as possible. The mash can had boiled and I enjoyed a nice hot cuppa on the way back down the branch to Derby. It felt like I'd used all eight weeks of training in one day, but it had been a unique learning experience. As we passed through the station for the second time that day, the train spotters were no doubt wondering why a half naked guard was now flapping his clothes out of the brakevan!

Steel
The one steel job that Derby retained was the 1211 Brierley Hill. It originated from the Eastern Region and was worked DOO (Driver Only Operated) to Derby, where it would be relieved by a driver and guard. After progressing through Burton-upon-Trent and Tamworth, the train would be turned across at Water Orton, to cut through the seemingly endless expense of Sutton Park. After negotiating Walsall, it would then continue along the South Staffordshire Line to the steel terminal at Brierley Hill. The job was essentially a trip working, where wagons were either picked up or dropped off at different sidings along the route. For instance, on its return from Brierley Hill, it would often be tasked to collect wagons from Round Oak or Wednesbury. Gaining access to Wednesbury Steel Terminal could be quite interesting at times. To enter the sidings, the train was required to propel, virtually blind, up a steep gradient. This wasn't always easy, particularly if you were trying to shove a heavy train on wet rails! With the engine (usually a Class 37) in reverse and the power handle wide open, the driver and guard would be desperately straining out of the cab windows, whilst the signalman in Wednesbury box would be shaking his head!

Bringing The Mail
Derby Trainmen had a bit of an on-off relationship with postal trains. Sometimes the work seemed regular, then other times it disappeared from the links completely. When I first started at Derby, there was an afternoon job, which required a guard to travel passenger to Lincoln and work a parcels train back. The job itself was straightforward enough, but the guard would have to wait around at Lincoln for about four hours before his return working appeared. This wasn't necessarily a bad thing however, as a stroll around the shops, a meal, a visit to the Cathedral, or even a pint or two could be most pleasant on a summer afternoon…before the rules regarding drinking on duty were strictly enforced!

16

The Lincoln parcels seemed to vanish around the end of 1990, and there was no other postal work for trainmen until early 1993, when a night job appeared. This time the guard, signing on at 2122, would travel passenger to Birmingham New Street and work a TPO (Travelling Post Office) train back. There would be around an hour's wait at Birmingham before the TPO arrived, then the post office staff would rush around it like ants, loading and unloading mail sacks before its next scheduled departure. Once this frenzied activity had died down a little, the postmen would then begin sorting the mail in the carriages, whilst the guard checked the train and advised the driver of the load. After a brief scheduled stop at Burton-upon-Trent, where more mail sacks were hurriedly thrown off and on, the train would continue to Derby, arriving around midnight. The guard would return to 4 Shed, but with less than four hours on duty, he would have to sit spare in the mess room for a while…the TCS was usually wise to any disappearing acts the trainman may have up his sleeve!

Research & Specials

British Rail Research based at the Railway Technical Centre (RTC) in Derby, provided a regular flow of work for 4 Shed. Along with track recording and gauging trains needing to be dragged here, there and everywhere, there were also periodic engine and rolling stock tests carried out at the Old Dalby test track in Leicestershire. This was the one and only road I avoided signing, simply because I found the work dull and repetitive in the extreme! If I had a preferred research job, it was taking the track recording train (in transit) to Crewe, then returning back pass, or vice versa…nice and straightforward! Trains were prepared or stabled in the Research Sidings situated near Derby PSB (Power Signal Box), and as most of these had to be propelled in and out, this place could be a difficult and exceptionally dangerous area to work in…a fact tragically demonstrated by the death of a shunter there one day.

A pair of 20s at London Road Junction. Note the RTC sidings on the left, and the entrance to the Carriage Works on the right, as previously described. Photo: P. Helme, circa 1989.

Occasionally the odd special working would come along, and in my short career at Derby, I got to work the Orient Express, a steam special, and even the Royal Train...albeit empty stock! There were also officer specials, which involved dragging an observation carriage full of railway hierarchy around a particular area. These were often exaggerated affairs, but could occasionally yield a bonus. They sometimes had their own gourmet chef aboard, so once the job was over, the train crew would be straight in scouring for any leftovers! Another job I ended up with was preparing a train for use in a joint emergency exercise. Using condemned carriages, a spare truck from the fire brigade, and several actors with made up injuries, a simulated rail accident was staged in Belper Goods Yard. The scenario was that a train had hit a lorry loaded with toxic chemicals and the resulting carnage would have to be dealt with by the three emergency services. Two crash test dummies played the part of the train crew...although at times, it was difficult to tell which were which! The dummy driver was left in the cab, whilst the dummy secondman was unceremoniously thrown down the embankment, to be accounted for later...the irony was not lost on me!

Emergency exercise at Belper Goods Yard. Photo: J. Riley 1993.

2. Sitting Spare

Endless comings and goings, timesheets being filled in, the inevitable practical jokes, lively chatter punctuated with frequent shouts of "Who's mashing then?" These were some of the activities that constituted life in 4 Shed Mess Room, and this is where you spent the majority of your time if you were booked spare! When I started at Derby, all that remained of the original No 4 Shed was the locker room, stores, several offices accommodating the TCS, roster clerk and union staff, and the mess room itself. To be honest, the facilities were pretty grim and would be considered largely unacceptable by today's standards, but the place was living history. Generations of enginemen had come and gone and only the walls remained to mark their passing and echo their shouts. When you were at 4 Shed, you really felt like another link in that historic chain, part of something larger and ultimately enduring.

The remaining buildings of Derby 4 Shed, Mar 1992. The mess room is situated to the far right. Photo: Author.

The nature of railway work demanded some rather unique hours of duty and the mess room essentially became like a second home. You can name any time on the 24-hour clock and I can safely say, as can most railwaymen, that over the years, I've signed on or off duty at all of them. 0226, 1443, 2312, you saw the job at all times of the day and night, in all seasons, weathers, moods…and political climates! Perhaps it's just the passing of time, but life seemed simpler then. There seemed much more light heartedness…before the world went completely crazy! Spare men would sit outside during the long summer evenings; some would wash their car on a Sunday, if things were quiet. Darts, cards, gambling, pin ups, fast cars, moderate drinking, all general bloke-type revelry, none of which was frowned upon because you were a man in a man's world, and it was okay…the job got done and life made a lot of sense! Everything revolved around the simple pleasures of tea, tobacco, tall stories, and the sharing of a common bond. If the mess room was like a second home, then many of the people became an extension of your family, simply because of the amount of time spent there.

The three most commonly used items in the mess room were the large communal teapot, the fruit machine, often referred to as the "Bandit", and the hotline from the TCS to the mess room. This was situated on the top shelf nearest the door. It would ring numerous times during a shift, primarily to inform relief crews that their trains were approaching, or that the Shed Men were required...or that a job had just been found for one of the several bodies sitting spare! Occasionally, someone would lift the receiver and pretend they were talking to the TCS. Everyone would be too busy chatting to realise the phone had never actually rung, so some unwitting individual would be dispatched on a fictitious errand, only to return later, rather red-faced!

The interior of 4 Shed Mess Room, Feb 1992. Photos: Author.

Spare turns were an inevitable but necessary part of train crew rosters, giving management a flexible framework in which to allocate personnel. At most depots there were two shifts alternating between days and nights. You wouldn't normally see many people from the other shift, unless you'd swapped turns with one of them, or happened to be in the mess room during the crossover periods, i.e. midday or midnight. According to your current position in the link, you were either on a booked job, or spare. If you were spare, the signing on time was often only a guide, as you could be moved two hours either side of it. For example, if you were 0700 spare, you could be deemed fair game for any jobs that fell between 0500 and 0900, if the booked trainman didn't show...provided you signed the road of course! For the most part though, you'd simply have to resign yourself to many a long hour in the mess room.

I was fortunate in some ways, because I gained fairly comprehensive road knowledge within a short space of time and could undertake most trainman jobs that came along. This kept my spare turns to a minimum, but even I began to succumb towards the end of 1992, when our work began to dry up. The only advantage to being spare was that after six hours, you could ask the TCS if he still required you. If he didn't, it was generally understood that you could go home and still get paid for eight hours. This goodwill worked both ways however, as you could be asked to stop and cover a job into overtime, if the need arose.

TRAIN CREW ROSTERS

BRITISH RAILWAYS   Region   B.R. 32711/3

Commencing ....19......

SUNDAY		MONDAY		TUESDAY		WEDNESDAY		THURSDAY		FRIDAY		SATURDAY	
On Duty	Turn/Dia No	On Duty	Turn/Dia No	On Duty	Turn/Dia No	On Duty	Turn/Dia No	On Duty	Turn/Dia No	On Duty	Turn/Dia No	On Duty	Turn/Dia No
		0800	400	0800	400	0800	400	0800	400	0800	400		
W		1700	TA	1700	TA	1700	TA	1700	TA			1945	F 1420
		BR/F		0915	440	0915	440	0915	440	0915	440		
						1400	TA	1400	TA	1400	TA	1945	R
		0800	480	0800	480	0800	480			0800	480	0800	1480
W		2200	TA	2200	TA	2200	TA	2200	TA			2100	1425
		0700	421	0700	421	0715	435R			0700	421	0700	1422
		1500	422R	1500	422R			1500	422R	1500	422R	1905	1432
		0200	TA	0200	TA	0200	TA	0200	TA	0200	TA		
W		1500	TA	1400	403	1500	422			1500	TA	1745	1433
		BR/F		0700	TA	0700	TA	0715	435	0715	435		
						1600	TA	1600	TA	1600	TA	1745	1435
		0805	453	0805	453	0805	453	0805	453	0805	453		
W		1400	TA	1400	TA			1400	TA	1400	TA	2045	1436

An extract from the Trainman's Link, circa 1992. Note the amount of spare turns by this time!

Turning HSTs

I found nights difficult at the best of times, but spare turns on nights were particularly soul-destroying. Some people preferred nights, but I always tried to swap mine for afternoon starts where possible, to remain with my own shift. Sometimes this wasn't possible, so I would have to endure a week of 2200 spare, or some similar delight! During those dead hours, my stomach would grind away, not knowing if it wanted breakfast, lunch or tea, and the longer I sat in the mess room, the less I felt like doing anything. Invariably, you'd end up with a job after about five hours, which was most unwanted! A typically irksome task that seemed to crop up regularly on nights was turning HSTs at Branston Junction. Basically, the job entailed taking the necessary HST set from Etches Park into the station. Once in the station, its second class section would be leading, i.e. behind the lead power car as it heads towards London St. Pancras, and the purpose of the job was to ensure that the first class section would be leading. This was achieved by using Branston, Birmingham Curve and Leicester Junctions, which formed a triangle just beyond Burton-upon-Trent. The work was undemanding enough, but after five hours, it was the last thing you wanted to do when your bed was almost within reach! The trainman would ride down in the rear power car (first class end), and stop the driver once clear of the shunt signal at Branston. He would then give the signal to set back and remain in that cab, ready to apply the emergency brake if necessary, as the driver propelled round to Birmingham Curve Junction. Once the driver was behind the main aspect there, he could proceed round to Leicester Junction and continue back to Derby. The trainman could join him up front, but would usually remain in the back cab, or the train itself. If the coaches hadn't been cleaned yet, he'd probably be scouring them for any booty! Newspapers and magazines were a favoured commodity during a long night in the mess room, but one of those well-travelled cheese sandwiches from the buffet car was best left alone! As the HST pulled into Derby, its first class section would now be leading, ready for its next departure to London. As St. Pancras is a terminus, all those hurried executive types travelling first class would now be able to exit the station first as well, but I wonder how many of them appreciated the process involved…it was just one of the many little jobs carried out during the early hours which made their world go round!

Ready for service. A HST awaits its next duty in Derby Station, circa 1993. Photo: R. King.

Being spare on days was more bearable, especially if there happened to be a good crowd in the mess room. Almost everyone took their turn at mashing in the communal teapot, so there was a brew on at least every hour. Practical jokes were virtually a way of life, and more importantly, helped to relieve much of the boredom. There were the usual gags of salt in the tea, which eventually progressed to chilli powder! Another favourite was exploding cigarettes, and trainmen with plenty of time on their hands would usually manufacture one or two! Two match heads would be wrapped in silver foil and placed in the end of a cigarette. The cigarette would then be placed in a pack and left conveniently on the nearest table. Usually the gag was meant for a particular individual, but as railwaymen and magpies share similar traits, practically anyone could get caught! Sometimes the pack would be completely forgotten about…until a brief, but unmistakeable, flaring up noise was heard, immediately followed by a startled curse! One habitual "cigarette cadger" who always took the last one from a pack, then proceeded to compound his crime by emptying the loose tobacco flakes onto the nearest person's head, once fell victim to the mother of all exploding cigarettes! One day, he helped himself to a cigarette from the trainman's table as usual, but unbeknown to him, this one had been specially prepared! The devious mastermind who'd arranged it obviously harboured some deep-seated grudge against the "cadger" because this one contained a lot of match heads! On his second drag, the cigarette flared up like a roman candle, conveniently removing all his nostril hair! He spent the rest of the day with a scorch mark on his upper lip, politely declining any further offers of cigarettes…an effective way to quit perhaps?

Each year, a small Christmas tree was set up in the mess room, but even this sacred symbol of peace and goodwill to all men wasn't exempt from use in practical jokes. After sitting for six hours, most spare men, on being given the TCS's permission to sign off, would quietly collect their things, bid their remaining colleagues a respectful farewell, and quickly depart, but one particular Trainman (G), on being given the "right away" seemed to positively delight in rubbing his remaining colleagues noses in it! Not content with this, he always wore large motorcycle gloves in winter (regardless of the fact that he'd never owned a motorcycle in his life), and had developed the rather unfortunate habit of whacking the person nearest the door over the head with them as he left! This was tolerated a couple of times, until one day he inadvertently left the offending items of clothing on the table whilst he went to obtain the TCS's permission to leave. His previous victims quickly filled the fingers of the over sized gloves with pine needles from the Christmas tree, and waited for his return. It wasn't long before he came swaggering back into the mess room, making the usual comments about leaving his colleagues to do all the work. He then grabbed his gloves, smacked the nearest person around the head with them and departed. There were a few glorious seconds of silence, then shouting could be heard outside, the nature of which seemed to relate to the mess room occupants' alleged illegitimacy! The gloves were targeted again the following winter, when they were filled with water and placed in the freezer overnight…I believe he started wearing a less conspicuous pair after that!

A Trip To Immingham

Sometimes, if you sat in the mess room long enough, some really unusual and challenging jobs would occasionally present themselves. I once had an unexpected trip to Immingham with a train of fuel tankers. Although it doesn't sound particularly thrilling, this was a real novelty for a trainman, as these jobs were normally driver only operated, and working to Immingham was virtually unheard of for Derby men. It was also very nearly a one-way trip for me, although I didn't realise this until we were well under way! Due to a malfunction, the Immingham driver had been forced to isolate the DSD (driver's safety device) in his cab, and according to the Rule Book, now required a secondman to ride with him. I was 1400 spare and had been sitting for a couple of hours when I was given the job. The TCS assured me that I would be relieved at Nottingham, so armed with this knowledge, I happily boarded the Class 37 which awaited me on the goods line with its train of tankers. I greeted the Immingham driver, whom despite the day's mechanical problems, seemed a pleasant enough chap.

As we approached Nottingham, the station appeared ominously devoid of people, especially those wearing railway uniform, so we ground to a halt at the end of the platform and I phoned the signalman to check on the whereabouts of my supposed relief. The signalman at Trent PSB was almost as much an accomplished con man as my own TCS! He informed that my relief was waiting at Lincoln…so on we went! I knew well before we even arrived at Lincoln that there was no relief scheduled. I was going the distance; it had just taken me a while to actually register the fact! It wouldn't have been so bad, but getting home could be a problem. My Immingham colleague knew of no return working until the following morning, and it was very likely that by the time we reached our destination, I would've missed the last passenger train as well. As we rattled on through Newark, Lincoln, and the dark territory as I called it, either side of Market Rasen, the fact that I could be stranded at Immingham began to sink in. This was developing into one of those legendary situations I'd often heard about, but never actually thought would happen to me…the possibility of 24 hours continuous duty! I would be joining the ranks of an elite few! At Wrawby Junction we joined the Cleethorpes line and continued on towards Brocklesby Junction, where we were finally routed into Imminghan Dock. The air became thick and heavy with the sweet stench of petrochemicals, and vast oil refineries lined each side of the track with their complicated network of pipes. A relief crew were waiting for us at the depot, and I reported to the TCS, who confirmed my worst fears…I was in fact stranded, at least until morning!

I made myself as comfortable as possible in the unfamiliar mess room, whilst trying to come to terms with the long night that lay ahead of me. I had about six hours in at this stage, so by 0500 first light, my total would be nearer fifteen. Add another three for the return journey, and

I'd be up to eighteen! This of course, was the best case scenario. If there was no return working at 0500, my total would rise still further. I was just contemplating this big pay day, when the TCS suddenly appeared. Apparently there was a job about to depart towards Cleethorpes, which was in the wrong direction as far as I was concerned, but I could "bail out" at Habrough Station, on the slim chance that the last passenger train hadn't yet gone. This was a gamble because if it had already departed, it would mean a cold night on the platform for me. There was a possibility of getting as far as Lincoln though, and as Immingham offered very little inducement to hang around, I boarded yet another Class 37 with a train of tankers, and we snaked around Brocklesby Junction again towards Habrough. As soon as I set foot on the platform, I consulted the timetable, and much to my relief, the last passenger train was on its way...I'd made it with about five minutes to spare! I had gone from a potential 24-hour duty, to a mere ten hour shift...which was fairly commonplace for me!

By sheer good fortune, this last Sprinter service was going all the way to Derby, and to my surprise, it was one of our drivers at the controls...I'd forgotten that Derby still retained the Grimsby and Cleethorpes work! I think the driver was more surprised than me, because I was the last person he was expecting to see at such a dark and lonely outpost, so far from home! For my part, I was just glad to see a familiar face and be heading in the right direction! There were only a handful of passengers aboard, whom according to the conductor guard, were all getting off at either Lincoln or Nottingham. This pleased the driver somewhat, as provided no one else wanted to get on, he could rattle through the multitude of little stations on the route without stopping...and possibly make last orders at his local! We slowed through every station, just to make sure no one was waiting, but otherwise hammered through the dark territory. There was nothing out there except fields, farm crossings and the odd lonely signal box. We were just getting used to having the road in our favour and flying past all the green signals, when we were suddenly checked. The driver reduced speed accordingly and we were eventually brought to a stand at a red signal. It was an unusual place to be held, so on behalf of the driver I got straight on the phone. The signalman informed me that trains in both directions were being slowed, as apparently a patient from a nearby secure hospital had escaped and the police were scouring the tracks for him at that very moment! I could see the foreboding building up on the hill with all its lights on. I could hear dogs barking and see torch beams sweeping back and forth. Suddenly, every tree and hedgerow harboured a madman waiting to pounce! Whilst my imagination was running riot, the signalman continued talking, but I wasn't listening. I was now feeling distinctly uncomfortable and was in a hurry to be off! It had the elements of a classic horror film; a lunatic makes good his escape by assuming the identity of a humble trainman...but perhaps there were enough lunatic trainmen around already, so no one would really notice! I returned to the safety of the cab as quickly as possible, and we proceeded at caution for the next 200 metres or so, before the driver opened up again...there was a pint somewhere with his name on it...or so he kept telling me! After successfully negotiating Lincoln and Nottingham, we finally pulled into Derby, and it was one weary trainman, with a few more grey hairs, who returned to 4 Shed that night!

The Run Round & Brake Continuity Test
A vital, but often overlooked aspect of any job, was the run round manoeuvre. This basically involved getting a train to face in the desired direction, by means of uncoupling the engine from one end, and re-coupling it to the other. Whether carried out in some far-flung corner of the network, or simply in the station yard, it was usually the trainman's responsibility. Allied with this duty came the brake continuity test, which had to be carried out whenever an engine was coupled to a train, or vehicles coupled or uncoupled. It didn't matter if the train was vacuum or air braked; the principle was essentially the same. After the trainman had hooked

on the coupling and connected the necessary brake pipes, the driver would then begin charging up the system, which would gradually release the train brakes. Whilst this was taking place, the trainman would walk to the end and put a tail lamp on the last wagon. Once the system was fully charged, he could then open the air cock, or disconnect the vacuum pipe on the last wagon. This exhausted the air, or destroyed the vacuum in the system, thus breaking the continuity and causing all the train brakes to re-apply. After checking the last three wagon brakes had functioned correctly (by kicking the blocks), the trainman would close the air cock, or replace the vacuum pipe, and the driver would recharge the system again. On satisfactory completion of the test, the train would be deemed fit to proceed.

As a result of accidents or engineering work, numerous freight jobs could be diverted via Derby, with some requiring to be run round in the station yard. It was on these occasions when a spare trainman would be called upon to undertake this duty and dispatch the various jobs on their onward journeys. The most memorable one I did was perhaps the Corby/Lakenby steel coil train, one grey, showery day. Each coil weighed in at approximately 25 tonnes (or so I was told), and there were three or four on each wagon. As I proceeded towards the end of the train to perform a brake test, I became aware of a definite increase in ambient temperature and an intermittent hissing noise! At first I thought there must be some problem with the wagons, until I realised the coils were fresh from the finishing mill! Although outwardly they didn't look hot, they were still radiating intense heat, and the intermittent hiss was the sound of raindrops hitting their surface and evaporating. I found out later that hot rolled coil (HRC) could be loaded straight onto the wagons at temperatures of up to 500 degrees centigrade!

St. Andrews & Sinfin

Not all run round jobs came uninvited, and my one off trip to Immingham wasn't Derby's only involvement with petroleum tanks. The Economac Oil siding at Derby St. Andrews had frequent deliveries of petroleum products from various refineries, and it was normally the spare trainman's job to run the train round in the station yard, or Derby North, before it was propelled into the siding. Most propelling movements into sidings were hazardous, but Economac was especially so. The track was curved and the driver unable to see any hand signals, so several rules had to be broken in order to successfully position trains in there. As had happened in so many sidings before, the person giving the hand signals could quite easily slip under the train and the driver would be completely unaware. With that in mind, I always adopted the procedure of standing well clear whilst the driver set back slowly. Once the train had been roughly positioned at the terminal, I would then partially dump the brake from the last wagon and stop him. It wasn't the most glamorous method, but it was certainly the safest!

Another less frequent job was the delivery of aviation fuel for the jet engine test beds at Rolls Royce. After being run round, this train would have to be taken down the Sinfin Branch to its discharge point at Sinfin Central. The branch was accessed via Melbourne Junction, approximately one mile west of Derby. As well as the Rolls Royce siding, there were also two small stations, and three ground frames to contend with. No1 and No2 frames operated the run round loop, whilst No3 frame controlled the entry and exit into the siding. After operating No3 frame, a loaded train could be propelled straight into the siding. Rolls Royce emptied the tanks as required, so the engine would either return to its home depot, or lay over at 4 Shed. Eventually the tanks would be discharged and an engine would be dispatched to collect them. This time, the accompanying trainman would have to employ all three frames, as once clear of the siding, the train would be propelled into the loop and the engine run round. Back in the station yard, it may have to be run round again, depending on its final destination!

The Wrong Kind Of Snow

In the absence of proper conductor guards at the station, spare trainmen were sometimes called upon to work passenger trains. Although I considered myself a freight guard through and through, working the occasional passenger train did offer some variety. One day you might be working a HST from Sheffield to London, the next, a Sprinter to Matlock, Nottingham or Crewe. We didn't issue tickets, collect any money, or really have much interaction with the passengers at all. We were there merely to operate the trains safely and in accordance with the Rule Book. To act as a passenger guard, trainmen still had to have the necessary road knowledge for a job, but also required additional training on HSTs, Sprinters and coaching stock...or slam door stock as it was often referred to.

In due course, trainmen received a day's instruction on each common class of Sprinter unit (Classes 150-158), and a day each on coaching stock, DMUs and HSTs. The training involved basic things such as preparation, fault finding, emergency procedures, and the operation of the automatic doors on the new Sprinter units. Emergency coupling was also covered, although this applied primarily to HSTs. They had two emergency couplings in each power car; one was a fixed bar for coupling two HST sets together, the other one was shorter with a pivoted head at one end for HST to loco coupling. We were given a traction manual to study beforehand, in which the coupling diagrams were notoriously difficult to follow, but after a practical demonstration, they really became self explanatory. Provided the HST towing eye had been fully extended and all the necessary locking pins were in place, the hardest part was probably getting the loco hook at the correct distance from the pivoted end of the bar, in order for it to be offered up and secured. Obviously, you couldn't stand between the buffers to facilitate this operation, so it took a few shunts to get exactly right. After which, it was simply a case of connecting the air pipes and any electrics, then performing a brake test.

An example of HST to loco coupling. Photo: R. King, 1991.

We were told that it wouldn't really be our job anyway, because in most cases there'd be a senior conductor aboard and it was his responsibility to prepare the emergency coupling...we were also told that one day pigs would achieve flight! The standard excuse always offered by "senior condoms" keen to avoid this particular duty, was that their £200 company issue suit would get dirty. The fact that they were issued overalls, as well as dry cleaning tokens, was beside the point! When a group of us learnt HSTs, we practised putting on the two different couplings in the sidings, never really expecting to have to do one for real. In fact, I think most trainmen probably went their whole career without having to do one, but I ended up with several during the winter of 1991. That was the year we had the "wrong kind of snow!" It may have been an unfortunate statement from a public relations point of view, but not altogether an incorrect one…it *was* the wrong kind of snow, compared to what we usually had! This stuff was unnaturally dry and powdery, almost like sand. It would barely stick together when compressed, but had an amazing ability to funnel into the engine compartments of HSTs and literally clog everything up. I'd certainly never encountered snow like this before and the HSTs seemed to be suffering because of it!

Definitely the wrong kind of snow! Photo: R. King, Feb 1991.

There was one particular day in February when it seemed like the entire HST fleet was succumbing to this unusual weather. I'd originally signed on duty at 1222 for the Denby job, but as it was cancelled, I ended up sitting spare. I didn't have to sit around for long though because I was immediately dispatched with a driver to go and rescue a failed HST near Moorthorpe Station. This was a London Newcastle service, which had already encountered problems with the snow and had now apparently given up completely. As there were still passengers on board we would have to work the service to Leeds, where it would be terminated. After being allocated a Class 47, we departed light engine from 4 Shed and proceeded rapidly northbound through Chesterfield, Sheffield and Rotherham, before being crossed over just before Bolton-on-Dearne Station. This enabled us to bypass the failed train and continue on towards West Kirby Junction, where we were crossed back over, then given permission to proceed into the occupied section towards it. As expected, the senior conductor hadn't prepared the coupling, or even carried out any detonator protection, and stood there looking rather useless in his £200 suit! I barely acknowledged him, for fear of saying something he'd regret…this was not a good start as far as I was concerned! I climbed into the guard's compartment of the lead power car and removed the access panel where the emergency couplings were stored…only to find none there! I would now have to trudge all the way down to the rear power car, in the hope that it's set would be intact. I was beginning to feel a little frustrated now, as I stumbled down the ballast with two hundred pairs of eyes glaring at me. Why had this train been allowed to enter service with vital equipment missing?

Why was the senior conductor unable to do his job properly? As I climbed into the rear power car, I noticed a passenger waiting at the guard's door. I knew he was about to make some enquiry regarding the train's delay, but as I wasn't in the best of moods at that moment, I pretended not to see him. That way, I wouldn't have to waste time answering foolish questions. Instead, I concentrated on removing the access panel with my T key. Unfortunately, all the square keyholes had been rounded off, rendering my key completely useless. As I struggled to get my fingertips behind the panel, I made the mistake of glancing over my shoulder at the passenger. He was just about to open his mouth, when rage suddenly overtook me! I tore the six foot panel off with my bare hands and threw it to the floor, then turned to him with what must've been a face like thunder! Whatever question he was about to ask, he thought better of it and scuttled back to his seat. Still seething, I grabbed the HST to loco coupling, hoisted its near 30kg weight onto my shoulder and speed marched to the other end! By the time I got there, the physical exertion had provided an adequate outlet for my anger and I was able to couple up without further delay. I did consider grabbing the senior conductor by the neck and giving him a vigorous shake, but instead, I gritted my teeth and returned to the rear power car to perform a brake test.

We were finally able to depart Moorthorpe and I resumed my role as secondman, whilst the senior conductor attended to his duties in the train…whatever they were! We then had a brief stop at Wakefield before terminating at Leeds. At least for the HST, it was only a short trip from there up to Neville Hill for attention, but for the remaining passengers, it was probably going to be a much longer journey. We were uncoupled by the station shunter and signalled into a vacant siding to await further instructions. My driver however, had other ideas and requested an alternative destination just around the corner…which became my one and only visit to Holbeck depot. Whether we actually sat in the official mess room or not, I don't know, but it certainly wasn't what I was expecting. It was more like someone's front room circa 1920s, and there was a distinct *Marie Celeste* feel about it! There was a kettle on the boil and a couple of vacant armchairs in front of a glowing coal fire. On an adjacent wall, a pendulum clock kept time with its constant but compelling beat. The place was empty apart from a cat, which gave us a questioning glance before returning to its slumbers in front of the fire. Spare men at 4 Shed often joked about who'd end up as the mess room cat, but now I had met the official, undisputed one, albeit at Holbeck! It was now almost dark outside, and the only thing required to complete the effect would've been gas lights! It was certainly a cosy environment in which to enjoy a cuppa, but it was all very surreal, and would've made an excellent episode of the *Twilight Zone*!

We were returned to the present rather abruptly when the phone rang and a distant voice on the other end instructed us to proceed to Neville Hill. After negotiating our way into the depot, it transpired that we would be returning to Etches Park with yet another failed HST. As we were eager to get under way as soon as possible, I coupled up for the second time that day and carried out a brake test, before obtaining permission to depart. The journey home was uneventful, and on arrival at Derby, we dragged the snowbound HST onto a vacant stabling road near Etches Park and returned light engine to the shed. I was expecting my other crew members from the Denby job to be long gone by now, but it turned out that they'd spent their afternoon and early evening rescuing HSTs as well!

Another one dragged in! Photo: R. King, Feb 1991.

New Accommodation
By the summer of 1992, a permanent pre-fabricated building had been erected on part of the car park, and the remaining bit of 4 Shed demolished. The fairly happy, settled period I had come to know was essentially over. Major changes were taking place, and they weren't all for the better. It was the beginning of the end when we moved into that new mess room…and I knew! The old ways were dead and I didn't like this humourless, sterile, politically correct way of working at all. As Derby lost more and more freight work, the true reality of sitting spare became painfully apparent.

The end of an era. Derby 4 Shed is demolished, Jun 1992. Photo: Author.

Apart from the continuing practical jokes and general tomfoolery to curb the boredom, the only real laugh I remember having in the new mess room was when about eight trainmen, myself included, were booked 0800 spare. At 1400, we were all anxious to get home, but no one had quite plucked up the courage to ask the senior TCS if they could go yet. If one was allowed home, then by rights, all the 0800 spare men could go, but no one wanted to be the first to ask…everyone was waiting for everyone else! Also, there were a lot of us and it would be a trifle indiscreet if we all went tramping out together, firing up our respective vehicles in the car park. (Trainmen were renowned for their old bangers, as opposed to the drivers in their sleek, high-powered models!) Eventually, someone decided to chance their luck and made their way along the corridor from the mess room to the TCS' office. Not wanting to miss any favourable response from the TCS, the other trainmen waited in the corridor, or pretended to read the notice boards in the lobby. As soon as the TCS gave the nod to this one individual, it was like a scene from The Great Escape! The signal was relayed from the trainmen in the lobby, to the many bodies waiting in the corridor, all with their bags and coats at the ready. It was an immediate mass exodus and the TCS could only stare in shock as they all trooped out. I think he had to check if there was anyone still in the mess room after we'd all gone! There was so much exhaust from all the cars starting simultaneously, that the Shed Men appeared, thinking someone had just arrived with a rake of Class 31s!*

These engines were not known for their environmental friendliness! With the demise of Class 20s, several pairs of 31s were regularly stabled at 4 shed. Usually they were left idling, but when started from cold, they belched out a thick fog of choking diesel fumes…so much so, that the station would not be visible from 4 Shed for several minutes!

3. Shed Men

Job Numbers: 480, 481 & 482

The phone would ring, then the same inevitable cry of "Shed Men!" would issue around the mess room. More often than not, you'd just started your snap, perhaps got into a newspaper or T.V. programme, or simply got your head down. Either way, the timing was always inconvenient, even if you were doing nothing…which was usually the case! Generally speaking, the shed job was the best one to have. By that, I mean it was marginally better than sitting spare, because at least you had some suggestion of usefulness to justify your presence in the mess room, and there was less danger of being sent off on some "dodgy" job! You also roughly knew the amount of work involved and could generally guarantee a finishing time. The other bonus was that rarely did you venture any further than station limits…although absolutely none of this could be relied upon!

I can count on one hand the amount of times I got the shed job at the weekend, but you could consider yourself lucky if it was your booked turn, or you just happened upon it by chance, because it meant missing out on any dubious ballast workings. Unless something drastic happened, you knew you could disappear after about six hours, whereas the ballast crews could be stuck in the middle of nowhere, often for unknown lengths of time (See Chap 5). Initially the signing on times for shed were the standard 0600, 1400 and 2200 shifts, and each turn could involve more than fifteen engine preparations and disposals, as well as other maintenance related tasks. In 1992, the signing on times were changed to 0800, 1600 and 0005…for reasons I never really understood? The job was adequately covered throughout the 24-hour period, why change a regular shift pattern to an irregular one? I personally thought it was done to make the job slightly less palatable and to cause further unsettlement amongst the workforce…but conspiracy theories weren't as popular then as they are now!

Once an engine arrived on shed, it would be left outside the fuelling point, a place commonly referred to as the wind tunnel! The TCS would then summon his shed men, and after a polite pause, the designated driver and trainman would trudge dutifully round to his office to receive instructions regarding the stabling of the engine. The roads primarily associated with shed moves consisted of the front and back roads through the wind tunnel, which were accessed via spring points permanently set in that direction. Next to the wind tunnel lay shed side, after which came three roads designated N3, N2 and N1 respectively. N3 was a through road and remained clear, whilst N2 and N1 were both stabling roads. Engines would arrive at various times throughout the 24-hour period, although the hours between 2000 and 0200 often generated the most activity. After consulting with the fitters (Mechanical & Electrical Engineers), the shed men would move the engine into the wind tunnel and shut it down, ready to receive fuel and water. Minor defects could be rectified at this stage, but if something more complex was required, or if the engine was scheduled for an 'A' exam, it would be moved onto the front road for further attention. Sometimes arriving engines would need to bypass the wind tunnel altogether and this was one of the occasions where the trainman would have to hold the spring points across whilst the driver carried out the move. Whenever I operated these points, there was always the fear in the back of my mind about momentarily losing grip of the lever as the engine passed through, thus causing one engine bogie to head in the direction of shed side, whilst the other would naturally head towards the wind tunnel…the result being a complete obstruction of the shed access! Fortunately it never happened to me, but it was certainly one way to stop the job!

Whilst fuelling and watering, the fitters would also clean the cab windows and marker lights. On completion, the shed men would restart the engine and continue through the wind tunnel and out over the N road head points. As the driver changed ends, the trainman would pull the necessary hand points for the desired stabling road. If there was a lengthy period of time before its next duty, the engine would be shut down and its battery isolation switch (BIS) taken out. Otherwise it would be left running, but in either case, its handbrake would be applied. During the night, HST sets also came through the wind tunnel for fuel and water, before returning to Etches Park Carriage Sidings via the station. No trainmen were required for this job…there weren't many hand points to pull! Nevertheless, the shed at night could become a hive of activity in a short space of time!

47845 receives attention in the wind tunnel, Aug 1993. Photo: R. King.

In theory, any driver could end up on shed, but most of the time a trainman would be paired up with a driver whom, for medical reasons, had been restricted to station limits, or jobs which always involved a secondman. Regular characters included the likes of Driver Welsh, Big Bill and Harry C, which often set the stage for many hours of lighthearted entertainment! As a new, inexperienced trainman, it did take a while to learn the ropes, and get used to certain drivers' idiosyncrasies. Some viewed you with complete contempt, whilst others couldn't do enough for you, but I found even the most cantankerous ones eventually came around in the end…given enough time! With engines waiting to be moved, and more coming onto the shed all the time, it made sense to share the driving duties. Trust was the key element, but this obviously took a while to earn. Some drivers explained the engines to you, showed you the necessary procedures and even let you drive under their supervision, so eventually you became experienced and trusted enough to move them on your own. The first engine I drove under such supervision was 47973 *Derby Evening Telegraph*, which for a young trainman just starting out, was quite a thrill! Even though the rules were severely stretched by allowing trainmen to drive, it was generally accepted as common practice and the only sensible way to get the job done…we were supposed to be future drivers after all! In time, many drivers were happy to lend you their key and remain in the mess room whilst you dealt with the engines, only to grudgingly appear if things suddenly became hectic!

It took me a lot longer to acquire the much sought after drivers' key though, and I only got one in the end because Harry C became fed up of me borrowing his! Nevertheless, I now had a key of my own and was able to operate on the shed effectively and with confidence.

A pair of 20s stabled on N1, adjacent to the wind tunnel. This picture was most likely taken at the beginning of 1992, as 4 Shed is still visible in the background, although the crane looks to be in the process of assembling the new train crew accommodation. Photo: Author.

I always enjoyed dealing with Class 20s whenever they appeared. Their cabs may have been a bit spartan and uncomfortable, and they were certainly showing their age by this time, but I found them to be good, solid, reliable workhorses with a unique character...not to mention a most agreeable engine sound! They were still the common traction on most of the Derby ballast jobs, being employed primarily on weekend engineering trains and trip workings, as well as the Chadd' shunt, and of course the Denby coal trains, although by the beginning of 1992, their appearances were unfortunately becoming less frequent. If there happened to be a pair of them in the wind tunnel, I would always commandeer them first, leaving a grumbling Harry C to deal with any other engines behind. Once the fitter had given the all clear, I would unlock the driving desk, move the controller from the off position to engine only, letting it prime for a few seconds, before pressing the start button and revelling in the throaty roar of the twin engines. The fitter would take cover as thick, acrid exhaust plumes filled the shed, then I would release the handbrake, energize the AWS (Automatic Warning System), un-peg the train brake, move the controller into the forward position, and finally, with one foot on the DSD pedal, release the straight air brake. Although it was bad practice, I just couldn't resist pulling the power handle right back in one move! At first nothing would happen, then there would be an ominous click as the relays kicked in. Within seconds, the engine noise would change from a passive tick over to that distinctive high-pitched cylinder thump, and then...lift off! I guess it was the railway equivalent of launching a Tomcat from an aircraft carrier! With stereo sound, I would power out of the wind tunnel, only to shut off rather quickly in order to negotiate the points outside! If you closed the power handle too sharply, there would be an unpleasant thump and a rather disturbing blue flash from the fuse box, so the trick was to close the power handle to notch one, then allow the engines to power down before shutting off fully.

If you'd planned it properly, you could coast quite happily right out over the head points, change ends, then set the other hand points for your required stabling road…pure magic! Stabling the engines was simply a reversal of the start up procedure, but if the engines were to be shut down, the BIS would have to be taken out on both locomotives, as well as the lighting switch. These were located outside between the bogies and resembled something from a Frankenstein film…big folding lever switches which sometimes emitted a spark to the unwary! When preparing 20s, I couldn't resist quoting the famous line "It's Alive!" as I re-engaged their BISs!

The driving controls of a Class 20, in this case 20088. Photo: R. King.

Class 47s were another favourite of mine and represented a good proportion of our shed work. They would arrive from all over the country, requiring attention after a hard day's labour. Although I was brought up with the traditional B.R. blue livery, I thought the new InterCity colours looked particularly smart. To see the wind tunnel at night, occupied exclusively by InterCity 47s was an impressive sight. I found them fascinating; where had they come from? What trains had they hauled? What sights had they seen along the way? I don't think there were many people who shared such a romantic view of them, but it was difficult not to like such a faithful class of locomotive…and attribute some sort of personality to them! It was quite easy really, especially when they were taking on water. Once their header tank was full, and without any regard to nearby personnel, they would blow the excess water through an overflow valve in their roof…just like a whale! The fitter would receive a cold shower if he was close, but it was almost as if the engine was trying to say "I've had a long hard day and I'm tired. Turn that bloody hose off and put me to bed!" I could see how Rev. Awdry had got some of ideas. Humans built these engines after all, why shouldn't they display some of our characteristics?

I don't know how much of an enthusiast Harry C was of 47s, because he fell victim to at least two humorous misfortunes with them on shed. The first happened when he and his trainman were tasked to move a pair of 47s from shed side. Quite logically, he dispatched his mate to the rear engine, whilst he climbed up into the other one. Obviously the plan was to drive off in opposite directions, but unfortunately, neither of them had realised the engines were coupled together. By amazing coincidence they both opened their power handles at the same time, only to find themselves in a tug of war contest…instead of a rope; it was two straining 47s! Realising there was some kind of fault, Harry shut of first, and as the coupling went slack, his engine ricocheted off the buffers of the other one several times. This caused him to lean out of the cab window and utter his usual catchphrase, which contained two expletives far too colourful to print here! The second occasion involved the classic engine shutdown prank. Harry would start up a 47, but unbeknown to him, his shed mate would sneak into the back cab and shut it down. A now concerned Harry would restart the engine, only for it to shut down again after a few seconds. Grumbling to himself, he would disappear into the engine room with his hand lamp to investigate the circuit breakers, before returning for a restart. By this time, his mate had sensibly vacated the back cab, because instead of colourful expletives, he'd probably end up with a clip round the ear! Harry would finally get under way, no doubt still grumbling to himself about awkward engines!

N2 and N1 occupied on night shed, Oct 1993. Photo: R. King.

Preparing engines was the responsibility of the driver, as trainmen were not deemed to possess the necessary technical knowledge until they'd completed their MP12 course. However, by observing the process often enough, I was able to do a basic engine preparation in an emergency…or if my driver had dodged off somewhere! After walking round the engine and checking its pipes, bogies, lights and any external gauges, it would be up into the cab to establish the status of the safety equipment. This involved flags, detonators, track circuit clips and fire extinguishers. Fuel and water gauges would be checked next in the engine room, along with the circuit breakers. After engaging the BIS, the engine would be started and the correct air pressures observed, before performing brake, power and DSD tests. It would then be a trip through the engine room, to conduct the same tests in the other cab. If you were really conscientious, both cabs could be swept clean as well!

Sometimes engines would need to be coupled together and this is where the trainman came into his own area of expertise. Donning his oily, full length orange smock and gloves, he would squeeze under the buffers, hook the coupling on and connect all the various pipes. 47s were straight forward enough, but 20s and 31s could have six different connections, including the vacuum pipe and the extremely awkward jumper cable…which often had to be knocked in or out of its socket with a brick! With all those pipes, space between the engines was at a premium, and as a result, there weren't too many overweight trainmen on the job!

Another duty of the shed men was to take 47s down to Etches Park for replacement brake blocks. It was one of those jobs that sounded straightforward enough, but could turn into quite an excursion at times! Once beyond the head points for the N roads, the engine would continue past the carriage sidings and into the shunt neck alongside the maintenance shed. Whilst the driver changed ends, the trainman would get the necessary clearance from the maintenance supervisor. Safety rules dictated that the supervisor had to warn his staff of any engine movements in the shed. This was achieved by him activating a series of blue flashing lights above the designated road, in conjunction with an audible warning…in this case, a two-tone siren! He had plenty of time to get his safety measures in place, because in order to get the engine from the shunt neck to the front of the shed, the trainman may have had to pull as many as eight different sets of hand points, whilst also keeping a good lookout for HSTs, and any other conflicting shunt movements…not to mention the multitude of trip hazards that littered the carriage sidings! Finally, the engine would be on the correct road facing the shed and the driver would change ends again, ready to drive in once the large roller shutter door opened. When it did, it was like entering the shuttle bay of the *Starship Enterprise*…flashing lights, sirens, and men in boilersuits looking busy! In order for the fitters to comfortably attend the engine bogies, the shed floor was roughly four foot below rail height, so once the engine was safely inside, there was a good ten foot drop for the train crew to overcome! The supervisor was most adept at operating his disco lights, but when it came to appearing with the set of portable steps, his record was not so good! The sight of Big Bill hanging from the engine handrails at full extent, his legs kicking in mid air, was not a pretty one, so the often younger, more agile trainman would perform the aerial acrobatics and eventually retrieve the steps. Re-blocking an engine could be a lengthy process, so the shed men would walk back to 4 Shed Mess Room…to await their next call!

4. Shunt & Trip Work

The Chadd' Shunt (T89)
Job Number 435 / Rostered 7hrs 35mins

In order to receive the full trainman's salary, new starters were encouraged to sign for their first road as soon as possible…and Chaddesden Sidings was usually it! Situated towards the north end of the station and around Chadd' curve, eight roads constituted the Civil Engineers tip sidings, shared in part with Steetley Construction. Just to confuse things however, the through roads were numbered 1 to 7, whilst the dead end cripple road was designated 6a!* As a full train crew were required for this job (i.e. a driver, secondman and guard), a novice trainman could act as secondman and learn the ropes fairly quickly, usually signing for the job within a matter of days. *(There was also an outside road, separate from the main body of the sidings.)

A pair of 20s was the usual form of traction, but these stalwart engines were eventually replaced with a single Class 31, which just didn't have the same appeal to me! After signing on at 0715, the crew would depart light engine from 4 Shed, and on the brief journey through the station yard, Slums Sidings and its associated ground frame would be passed on the right. Signing for Chadd' also included this little enclave, but on querying the frame with the other crew members, the standard response was elicited, " Don't worry, you'll never have to go in there." To be fair, I only had to go into Slums Sidings about three times in four years, so I guess they were half right! At least four roads at Chadd' were always occupied with ZCV (Clam) ballast wagons, so unless an empty road had been left preset, the guard would have to pull the necessary hand points for the engine to proceed down to the shunter's cabin at the far end of the sidings. There were at least two shunting staff permanently based here, and after consulting with them about forthcoming operations, work would either commence in earnest, or everyone would retire for a cuppa…it was very often the latter!

The T89 and T91 engines stabled on N1, awaiting their next shunt and trip duties. The lead engine is 20007. Photo: Author, circa 1992.

37

The Civil Engineers (CE) department was charged with the repair and maintenance of the railway infrastructure, with the majority of this work being carried out at the weekends, (See Chap 5). Engineering (or departmental) trains would arrive at Chadd' on Sunday, loaded with spoil from the various weekend worksites. These wagons would be unloaded during the week, with the spoil being reclaimed or used for landfill. By this time, the shunting staff would've received the weekly ballast circular detailing train requirements for the following weekend, so trains would be continually marshalled at Chadd' and other CE sidings, to meet these requirements. Trains would be set for unloading, empty wagons would need to be marshalled into trains to collect fresh ballast, wagons containing fresh ballast would have to be marshalled into weekend engineering trains as required, whilst crippled wagons would be shunted out accordingly. These were all typical duties carried out by the T89 engine and crew. Saturday was usually the busiest day for shunting, as last minute wagon changes, or even the complete re-marshalling of some trains may be required, before they all began disappearing to their respective worksites from early evening onwards. The guard was sometimes called upon to assist, but if there were two shunters present, they knew where they wanted things and normally conducted operations on the ground whilst the train crew remained in the cab. Things were more efficient that way, and besides, it was helpful to have as many eyes in the cab as possible once the shunting got under way!

31461 on shunting duties at Chaddesden Sidings, Mar 1992. Photo: Author.

Brake Sticks & Shunting Poles

To facilitate operations, most wagons were loose shunted, which meant the continuous train brake generated by the engine was not used. Wagons to be shunted from the train would be uncoupled and have the vacuum (or air) drained from their brake reservoirs, then once the engine had provided enough push, the idea was for them to roll towards their allotted roads by themselves. As there were no brake pipes to worry about, this enabled the shunting staff to couple or uncouple portions of the train using a shunting pole, which saved them from having to scramble under the buffers each time.

This vital, but unassuming piece of equipment was basically a wooden pole about eight feet in length with a metal hook at one end. To uncouple, the shunter would rest the pole on a buffer sleeve and position one end underneath the coupling. Using the sleeve as a fulcrum, he would then push downwards and flick the coupling off its draw hook. Coupling up required a little more skill and involved catching the dangling coupling with the pole hook and flicking it up onto the draw hook, again using the buffer sleeve for leverage. To have any success with the shunting pole, the couplings would have to be slack and the buffers squeezed up, so the train would very often still be in motion whilst these operations were carried out…which is why the pole was eight feet long and the shunter remained well clear of the buffers! The brake stick was a more substantial piece of wood, rather like a squared off baseball bat. It had a million and one uses, but perhaps not all of them were legal, or even railway orientated! Nevertheless, its primary function in life was to aid in the application or release of wagon handbrake levers. Forcing the levers down with the brake stick and securing them with a locking pin was the prescribed method of applying handbrakes, whereas pulling the pin whilst simultaneously giving the lever a smack with the brake stick, was the most effective way to release them. It could be quite a stress busting experience, walking the length of the train knocking off handbrakes!

Shunting wagons is a real art, and with the right crew all working as one, it could look like poetry in motion. Shunting with a pair of 20s was an unrivalled experience though, and it wasn't usually long before wagons were flying everywhere! The engines would be coupled onto a long string of unsorted wagons and the whole train would then have to set back round Chadd' curve, almost into the station yard in order to clear the sidings head points. All shunting movements were controlled by hand signal, and with a train nearly a third of a mile in length, it could be difficult to see the shunter at times, but once clear of the head points, he would raise both his arms indicating us to stop. There would be a brief pause whilst he set the required road and used his shunting pole to uncouple a portion of the train, before calling us forward. As the uncoupled portion had to be given enough momentum to proceed towards its allotted road on its own, his hand signal would become more vigorous if we weren't pushing quickly enough! In this case, the driver would open the power handle fully. At first there would be no response, then the engines would rapidly power up, increasing in noise and speed. Within seconds, the shunter would raise both his arms again and the driver would quickly close the power handle, whilst simultaneously applying the engine brake. There would be the characteristic dull thump as the engines powered down, as well as the occasional blue flash from the fuse box! The engines would initially come to a dead stand, but then the remaining wagon couplings would stretch out, hurling us another couple of feet! Anything not properly secured or wedged, including the guard and teapot, would be thrown forward, and the uncoupled portion of the train would be observed (hopefully) rolling towards its desired road, with the other shunter in hot pursuit! To retard and ultimately halt its motion, he would have to jam his brake stick under the nearest wagon leaf spring, using it as a fulcrum to press down on the handbrake lever with his full weight. Riding the brake stick was a dangerous practice and strictly against the rules, as it could easily snap, sending the unfortunate operative under the wheels! Nevertheless, once the wagons had been positioned satisfactorily, the shunter would signal the driver to set back again to repeat the procedure. In this way, a long string of wagons would be sorted, crippled wagons removed, and individual trains marshalled on their designated roads.

Off The Road

If only one shunter was available, he would continue to work his magic with the shunting pole whilst the guard operated the hand points as required. The shunter would shout which road to set for the next move, so it was imperative for the guard to remember how the roads were numbered! It was all very well standing at the head points and hearing the shunter shout 7, but if you counted across from 1 to 7 and forgot to include 6a in your calculations, then the result could be quite devastating…particularly since 6a had stop blocks about half way down it! This was the probably the easiest way to slip up, but with loose shunting, there were other less obvious ways. Once when I was the secondman, we'd just sent a raft of six wagons down one road, when the shunter called a halt for a tea break. Thinking these wagons would have their motion arrested by the already stationary wagons on that road, we trundled past them on an adjacent empty road to the cabin. All the through roads converged near the cabin and we sat there waiting for the pot to boil. As I was reaching for my cup, I just happened to glance out of the side window and see a long string of wagons heading straight for us! The loose wagons had collided with the stationary ones, which obviously hadn't been secured properly because they were now all heading our way! There was no time to do anything as they were already on top of us, so I simply told my driver to hold onto something as we were about to be hit! Thinking I was joking, he laughed, but in the next second, there was an almighty crash and he was literally thrown from his chair! The wagons were perhaps only travelling about five miles an hour, but they hit us with a force of several tonnes. The impact caused the last two wagons to become derailed, but fortunately the damage to the engine was minimal and the only injury sustained was one of the driver's more sensitive areas being scalded with tea!

Although Chadd' prepared many of the trains used in the repair and maintenance of the region's tracks, its own sidings left a lot to be desired. Most of its tracks and points were in a poor state and with a combination of wooden sleepers and loose chairs, it made the roads especially prone to spreading. This is where the rails are pushed wider apart and the wagon or engine wheels fall between them, causing the train to become derailed. Much as it might come as a surprise to the Railway Inspectorate, or some health and safety statistician, having wagons off the road at Chadd' was fairly commonplace, but often easily remedied amongst ourselves without involving any paperwork…the loading shovel was usually employed to re-rail any errant wagons! However, on one occasion the engine itself became derailed and the breakdown crane had to be sent for, so there was no avoiding the subsequent reports…or "please explain" forms, as they were called!

The Driver's Slip

Even though the majority of its work was carried out in the sidings, T89 was still classed as a trip working and was therefore often dispatched to collect or deliver wagons from other places as required. A regular destination was Sandiacre Ballast Sidings situated in Toton Yard. If a train had to be taken, it would no doubt be marshalled during the course of the morning, and once shunting had ceased for the day, the guard would couple the engine to it. Walking down one side, he would then check couplings and handbrakes, before placing a tail lamp on the last wagon and performing a brake test. The checks would be repeated up the other side of the train, and once back at the engine, a driver's slip would have to be made out. Whenever an engine was coupled to its train for the first time, or a train's configuration altered en-route (i.e. loaded, unloaded or shunted), a driver's slip would be required for its on-going journey. This is where the guard has to complete a standard form detailing the characteristics of his train, matched against the route it will be taking. Limits for a particular route would be obtained from a freight loads book and entered on the left (authorised) side of the slip. The guard would then have to consult his Working Manual (white pages), or the information table painted on each wagon, to calculate his train's length, weight, speed, etc, before entering them on the right (actual) side of the slip. Provided the figures in the actual column didn't exceed the ones in the authorised column, the train would be deemed fit to proceed and the slip handed to the driver.

DRIVER'S SLIP

To be handed to DRIVER before commencement of journey

Date _____ Locomotive/s Class/es _____

W.T.T No _____

Time _____ From _____

To _____

AUTHORISED		ACTUAL	
Basic Load (tonnes)	☐	☐	* Actual Load (tonnes) Or
* Maximum Load (tonnes) Or	☐		* Actual No. of M.G.R. Wagons
* Authorised No. of M.G.R. Wagons			* Delete wording not applicable
+ _____ Brake Force for Basic Load (tonnes)	☐		
+ _____ Brake Force for Maximum Load (tonnes)	☐	☐	Brake Force Available (tonnes)
+ Insert Brake Force Category			
Route Availability R.A .No.	☐	☐	Highest R.A. No. on train
		☐	No. of wagons
Length Limit (S.L.Us)	☐	☐	Actual Length (S.L.Us)
		☐ M.PH.	MAXIMUM TRAIN SPEED Maximum speed of slowest wagon in train; subject to strict observance of any lower temporary or permanent speed restriction which may be in force on the route taken.

SEE OVER FOR PARTICULARS OF 'DANGEROUS' GOODS FORMED IN THE TRAIN

Depot _____

Signed _____ Grade _____

A trip to Sandiacre was straightforward enough, but in theory T89 could be sent to any CE siding in the region. Although it was rare to venture much further than Toton, we did occasionally get sent to places as diverse as Burton, Loughborough, Stoke and Gloucester, which is why proper road learning was essential. In most cases, if the booked guard didn't sign the road, the secondman sometimes did and was able to conduct.

Waiting Time

Most of the time, the day's shunting would be completed within a couple of hours, and if there was no scheduled trip to Sandiacre or anywhere else, that was basically it! The engine and crew couldn't just return to 4 Shed though. They had to justify their existence and would have to hide round at the sidings until at least six hours had elapsed. If it became apparent that there was going to be several hours of inactivity, the engine(s) would be shut down and the teapot put to good use, or the crew would all suddenly turn into those toy dolls...the ones whose eyes automatically shut on any angle less than perpendicular! It isn't often long though before enginemen with time on their hands get up to some sort of mischief, and one particular day I definitely played an ace!

I had been the guard all week and we'd been quite busy, shunting here and tripping there, but in all that time the secondman had never lifted a finger to assist me...the fact that he was a relief driver had a lot to do with it! A relief driver was basically a trainman who'd successfully completed the driving course and could now undertake the odd driving turn, usually nothing more than a sprinter to Matlock, Nottingham or Crewe though. In between these occasional driving turns, they still had to undertake normal trainman duties, but now they'd taken another step towards becoming a registered driver, many refused to sign

41

anywhere that involved any sort of guard duties or getting their hands dirty. That being the case, they were either consistently booked as secondman, or spare, which would leave them conveniently available for any possible driving turns. As a driving turn involved a higher rate of pay, many relief drivers could be found skulking in the mess room with the faint glimmer of pound signs in their eyes! Our secondman was no exception and at present, was sat in the shunter's cabin with his feet up. The driver and I were still in the engine, when the shunter climbed aboard and remarked on his laziness, and how something should be done to get back at him. Cab phones hadn't been introduced long and were still very much in their infancy, but our engine had been fitted with one and I think the shunter and I noticed it at the same moment. It was obvious from our devious grins that we'd both arrived at the same conclusion…it was time for a call! He gave me the number of his cabin, which I duly phoned. It was possible the secondman would ignore it, but surprisingly he answered and I had to quickly effect the gruff, matter-of-fact voice of our senior TCS. Trying desperately not to laugh, I told him that he was needed for a driving turn and to report back to the shed straight away. My voice had been so unrealistic, that never for a second did I actually believe he'd fallen for it, so I put the phone down and tried to think of something else instead. I had however underestimated a relief drivers' avaricious nature, because suddenly the cabin door flew open and the secondman emerged, hurriedly pulling on his coat and signalling to us to pick him up. Rubbing our hands with gleeful delight, we pretended not to understand his wild gesticulations, so bag in hand he began running towards us!

"Look at this…it's the quickest he's moved all week," laughed the shunter.

Just as he was about to reach the engine, the driver put it in reverse and crept back slowly, making him run that little bit further. Eventually he caught up with us and I leaned out of the window.

"What's up, have you had a phone call?" I enquired innocently.

"Yes, I've got to get back to the shed immediately" he gasped between breaths.

"Was it the TCS?" I asked.

"Yes, come on, let's go!"

"No it wasn't…it was me!"

I watched as the realisation gradually sunk in, then he grabbed a handful of ballast and began throwing it at the cab. The driver and shunter were beside themselves, mainly because the secondman would've climbed up and throttled me if he hadn't been so out of breath! When we were next paired together, he got me back by re-arranging all the pages in my Rule Book and Working Manual, stripping the battery and bulb from my hand lamp, and secreting the entire contents of my bag all over the sidings. I didn't mind too much, as I'd already taken the liberty of hiding a metal fishplate in his bag. These weighed about four kilos and I believe he carried it around for two weeks before realising…happy days!

The 91 Trip (T91)
Job Number 440 / Rostered 8hrs

Most of the fresh ballast for the weekend engineering (departmental) trains, was brought into Chadd' by the 91 Trip. Signing on at 0730, another full train crew would depart 4 Shed in a pair of 20s (latterly a 31), and practically follow the Chadd' shunt engines round to the sidings. Whilst the T89 engines and crew waited at the shunter's cabin, the guard from T91 would couple up and prepare his train of empties for their journey to Mountsorrel. This was the Redland Aggregates siding situated between Loughborough and Sileby, although I believe the quarry itself was nearer Barrow upon Soar and the ballast was conveyed to the siding. On arrival at Sileby Junction, the train was required to propel into Mountsorrel, which I always considered to be an exceptionally dangerous move. For a start, we had to propel across both

42

main lines, which I found a little unnerving, particularly since HSTs rocketed up and down close to 100mph...I could only imagine the devastation if the signalman ever forgot we were there! The other worrying factor was that we were also propelling into Mountsorrel virtually blind! There were often two trains already in the siding, and as our train snaked across the junction, it always looked as though we were on a collision course with them. The signalman wouldn't let us set back until the shunter had set an empty road and confirmed it of course, but propelling into that siding always seemed like an act of pure blind faith to me! Due to the angle and length of train, there was no possible way to see where you were heading...until it was too late! Unfortunately it took the death of yet another yard operative before other people realised this danger and operating procedures were changed.

Before the accident, the engine would be run round in the siding and the wagons dragged through the loader. The guard would then complete his brake test and driver's slip, and the train would be in order to return to Chaddesden. After the accident, the train had to continue passed Mountsorrel and run round at Humberstone Road Sidings, just before Leicester Station. On its return, it could then simply proceed straight into Mountsorrel, which was undoubtedly a lot safer.

Returning from Mountsorrel. 31126 heads the 91 trip at Trent Junction, Nov 1991. Note the handbrake lever and leaf spring on the ZCV (Clam) wagon, as previously described. Photo: R. King.

5. Weekend Ballast

The CE department either sub contracted or undertook the majority of infrastructure maintenance themselves, which could involve anything from a simple broken rail to large scale engineering works. In order to minimise disruption to passenger services, large-scale work was generally carried out at weekends, commencing Saturday night and continuing into Sunday. At a pre-arranged hour, the signalman would grant the engineers' possession of a section of running line. The majority of these possessions would be granted after the last passenger service of the night, or when services could be successfully diverted. This possession would last for a set amount of time, within which the necessary repairs had to be completed. Once a possession had been granted, its boundaries would be protected by detonators, lookout men, and illuminated marker boards. Worksites could then be established within these boundaries, under the control of an engineering supervisor. Provided the signalman maintained his safety measures, there should be no unexpected visitors! Only the scheduled engineers' (departmental) ballast trains would be allowed to proceed towards a possession, where they would wait at the marker boards for permission to enter.

A typical weekend engineering operation was re-ballasting, which basically involved sections of track being lifted and the old track bed removed. Fresh ballast would then be replaced, and the track re-laid. Depending on which stage the work was at, trains would either arrive empty to be loaded with spoil, or with fresh ballast for re-laying…or a combination of the two. At the worksite, most of the necessary plant, personnel and equipment would already be in place, which in itself was an impressive logistical operation, so all the train crew had to do was turn up with the wagons and work to instructions. Although re-ballasting of some form or another constituted a large proportion of weekend work, other engineering jobs could include such things as cable laying, bridge inspections, cess clearance and tunnel repairs, and the trains would also bring some of the equipment to facilitate the task in hand. In each case, a full train crew was always required. Each weekend, there could be as many as eight different engineering jobs originating from Derby, so crews could find themselves scattered anywhere around the region. Leicester, Toton and some of the other remaining local depots also played their part in the work, whether providing trains and crews for their own allocated work, or relief crews for others. Up to 1992, the common form of traction for an engineering train was a pair of 20s, but as these were gradually withdrawn, a pair of 31s, or the odd 47 filled the void.

An engineers' ballast train had to be constantly manned throughout a weekend possession, so the train crew would normally be rotated over three shifts. For example, a crew signing on at 1900 Saturday would collect a train from Chadd' and take it to a particular worksite. The second crew, signing on around 0200 Sunday, would then be taken to the worksite by staff minibus or taxi to relieve the first. A final crew (if required) signing on around 0800, and also arriving at the worksite by motor transport, would relieve the second crew and eventually return the train to Chadd'. If you were scheduled to work, your booked time in the link usually determined which shift you ended up on. If you happened to be booked a Saturday rest day, you could opt to work this, as well as Sundays, for which a higher rate of pay was offered. In this case, the shift you ended up on was then governed by your next time on duty, as required periods of rest had to be observed.

Front End Or Rear End?

To be honest, weekend engineering trains were pretty undemanding for the train crew. Once in position at the worksite, the train was very often not required to move again for the remainder of the shift, so the hardest part was probably signing on at such anti-social hours in the first place, and then coming to terms with the sheer boredom that followed! The driver and secondman would reside in the front cab, whilst the guard remained in the back cab, regrouping occasionally for a periodic mashing! In theory, front and rear end turns were distributed evenly throughout the trainman link, irrespective of whether you were a Trainman (D) or (G). In practice however, this was rarely the case. During my first year at Derby, I was often booked as the secondman, but as my road knowledge and experience increased, and because I was consistently punctual, particularly during the small hours, I eventually reached a point where I was rarely considered for a front end ballast turn anymore. The relief drivers and other assorted shirkers thought they were getting one over on me, but this scenario suited me just fine. Once the initial guard duties had been completed, I preferred to be on my own in the back cab. That way, I was guaranteed not to have to endure any potentially frustrating company…except my own of course! Neither did I have to invent or engage in any pointless small talk, because even with a decent driver, the conversation topics eventually dried up. In short, I had the back cab all to myself and could set my stall out accordingly…I had peace in which to sit out the mind numbing hours until the relief arrived!

Saturday Night

Start times for a Saturday night ballast crew could range anywhere between 1800 and 2100, and after signing on, people would gather in the mess room and spend about fifteen minutes comparing their respective jobs, obtaining an adequate supply of water for the night, and perhaps more importantly, speculating on the approximate arrival time of their relief…then complaining to anyone who'd listen! Although the mood was light hearted, there was always a tiny bit of uncertainty as you departed, to who knows where for who knows how long! Not many people left the mess room without giving the shed men an envious glance either!

Saturday night ballast jobs all began the same way…light engine to Chadd' to collect the train! The guard would couple on and carry out the necessary checks before departure. As there were no lights in the sidings, this basically involved stumbling around the length of the train in relative darkness…depending on the season of course! In most cases, a TOPS (Total Operations Processing System) computer printed train list was available which incorporated a driver's slip at the bottom, so all the guard had to do was check the details and sign it, before handing it to the driver. The signalman would be informed and the train would then depart to its respective worksite, which could be just a few short miles away, or the other side of Northamptonshire. After departing Chadd', trains with a northbound destination had to be run round in the station yard first. Some trains were so long that the signalman had to talk them past DY449 (the starting signal on the Up Goods in the station). In this case, the guard would get on the phone and relay the signalman's instructions to the driver by hand signal. Once the last wagon had cleared the north end points, the signalman would inform the guard, who in turn would stop the train. He would then uncouple the engine and remain with the train, carrying out another brake test once the secondman had re-coupled at the other end.

Sunday Morning

Having been a labourer of some description for most of my working life, I was never envious of the platelayers at the worksite. It was hard enough turning up at these unsocial hours in the first place, never mind labouring through them, in all weathers, to meet a strict deadline. I'm sure many of them saw us sitting in our cab, sheltered from the rain and cold, and wished they could exchange places with us. However, like most things in life, our reality was often quite different. Sitting on a ballast job was essentially the same as sitting spare, except there were no comings or goings like there were in the mess room, and no potential for a change of scenery. A guard residing in the back cab could often go eight hours without actually seeing or talking to anyone…try and imagine how that'd feel next time you're in your own place of work! After a while, I began putting some of this dead time to use and completed a correspondence course in vehicle mechanics, started learning a second language, and even began writing notes for a future book! Of course the irregular hours played havoc with your body clock and digestive system, and from the idling locomotive(s), came the constant sweet, sickly smell of diesel fumes, which contributed further to this unhappy human condition. In effect, the whole experience was largely uncomfortable, unfulfilling and above all, mentally and physically debilitating, which in a perverse sort of way, was worse than any physical labour! Even sleep offered little release, and although enginemen have the reputation of being able to sleep anywhere, I never could…unless it was flat on my back in a bed! As much as I liked Class 20s, they were a damn uncomfortable engine to reside in for any length of time. The chairs were very basic, and most had no arm rests. The secondman or guard could rest his feet on the handbrake wheel in front of him, but with no other leg support, this position quickly became uncomfortable. Similarly, he could swivel his chair round and rest his legs on the driving desk behind, but this was a rather cramped position. I eventually resorted to placing my smock on the floor and stretching out fully behind the chairs, which was ideal for me. I can't say it was ideal for a certain guard who relieved me once though, because as he pushed open the door where my feet were, and began climbing up into the cab, I rose in the gloom like Dracula from a coffin. He had the shock of his life as our faces met just above floor level, so much so, that he fell off the steps with a near cardiac arrest! Class 47s were slightly more comfortable, but the high-pitched scream of the air compressor kicking in every 20 minutes had the potential to drive you insane after a while…which might explain a few things actually!

As the hours ticked slowly by, only three things remained foremost in the minds of a crew waiting for relief; what time do the relief sign on, how long will it take them to get here, and will they be able to find the worksite when they do? On paper, each shift roughly equated to eight hours on duty, but in reality, ten and twelve hours were commonplace. This was due partly to the fact that the relief timings rarely took into account the travelling times to and from a particular worksite. A crew stuck near Luton would obviously have a longer wait for relief, and subsequent journey back to 4 Shed, than a crew who had remained within a 20 mile radius of Derby. The timings also didn't take into account unreliable trainmen not turning up for duty in the small hours, delays with the motor transport, and the time it could take a relief crew to find some obscure worksite in the middle of nowhere!

Relief
Having a worksite on a main line and arriving by rail was simple. Trying to reach it by road in the middle of the night was something entirely different! For some of the more nondescript trackside locations, the taxi or minibus carrying the relief crew could spend a while travelling up and down dark country lanes, its occupants desperately scanning the surrounding area for any evidence of railway activity. As the vehicle may have changed direction several times during the search, eventual arrival at the site could be quite disorientating for the crew. In the absence of any distinguishing landmarks, or line side features, it could often be difficult to ascertain which direction the train was facing, and more importantly, if the job had been run round yet! If it hadn't, there was a distinct possibility that it would have to be done during your shift! Also, the train you were relieving could be in a cutting, on a viaduct, up an

46

embankment, or on rare occasions, in a tunnel. At the very least, the relieving crew would usually have to climb over a fence, or traverse a field in order to reach the track. The likes of Big Bill trying to squeeze himself and his provisions through a barbed wire fence at 0300 on a Sunday morning was always a highlight!

Just because a crew had been relieved and were happily ensconced in the minibus awaiting the journey home, it didn't necessarily mean all their problems were over. Some of the transport drivers had been on for hours, and the drink-driving rule wasn't always strictly adhered to by some of them either! Consequently, there have been many instances where transport drivers have nodded off whilst returning crews home. Once when we were on the M1 travelling back to 4 Shed from a job, our driver veered from the fast lane, right across to the hard shoulder and back again…a pretty clear indication that he'd fallen asleep at the wheel, woken at the last second, then drastically over compensated for his mistake! Fortunately, the traffic had been light at that time in the morning, but one Derby crew wasn't so lucky when their minibus overturned under similar circumstances. Although some of their injuries were quite severe, they were all fortunately able to return to work in due course.

A pair of 31s on an engineers' ballast train near Market Harborough. This photo was taken on a bright, clear Sunday morning, which doesn't really do my previous description of the grim early hours justice! Photo: R. King, circa 1993.

1745 Bedford
I think the most sought after ballast job on a Saturday night was probably the 1745 Bedford, which tended to crop up every so often. This was a nice straightforward run from Chadd' to Bedford, where the crew would be relieved in the station, before returning home on the next passenger. Its main attraction was the achievable and generally guaranteed finish time, but this depended entirely on the mood of the signalman at West Hampstead PSB, and the Bedford TCS!

There were few surprises to be had during the steady run to Bedford, although after Kettering, the train could sometimes be routed onto the slow line at Harrowden Junction (or Weetabix

Junction as it was sometimes called, since the factory was situated right next to the track), so if the guard hadn't been paying attention from the back cab, he would suddenly find his train temporarily diverging from the main lines after Wellingborough, to pass through Sharnbrook (or Wymington) Tunnel. Once over Sharnbrook Summit, the tracks would converge at Sharnbrook Junction again, but the train would continue on the Up Slow, where it would finally be held at Bedford North. Here the train would stand until the Bedford crew signed on, at which point, the signalman would finally allow it into the station for relief.

The waiting time at Bedford North could range between one or two hours, and was dependent on the relief crew signing on at the correct hour, and the time of the possession they were eventually working the train forward to. Although the Derby crew were booked to return home on a specific passenger train at a specific time, this didn't stop them from trying to get into Bedford straight away, in an attempt to catch an earlier service! Some people would be on the signal phone every half hour, asking if the train could be allowed into the station, whereupon it could be secured in one of the platforms, and everyone could then disappear on the next available train home! Although it probably only meant gaining two hours or so, it was the difference between finishing still within the boundaries of Saturday night, or the early hours of Sunday morning. It was often amusing to listen to the tone of these requests, from particular crew members who had a vested interest in finishing early…usually to catch last orders! They always began amiably enough, then degenerated into frustration, and finally threats of leaving the train, as more and more time passed by! Nevertheless, it *was* frustrating to be sat less than half a mile from your destination and watch each northbound HST pass by on its way back to Derby. To make matters worse, it was usually a Derby man at the controls, so he'd whistle up and make a drinking motion with his hand as he rocketed past! Once the train had been allowed to proceed into the station for relief, the previous frustrations were quickly forgotten, and the crew able to relax on the homeward journey. Although the job often only equated to a seven hour shift (which was exceptionally rare for a weekend ballast job), the booked passenger train stopped at most of the major stations along the route, and also called at Nottingham before finally pulling into Derby around 0030…which is why most of the crews tried to get an earlier, faster and more direct service!

There were a couple of occasions when the job wasn't always so clean cut though, usually because of staff availability at Bedford. Once, due to a clerical error, we arrived at Bedford to find no relief booked on, so we had to work the train forward to Cricklewood and stable it in the Recess Sidings. Ordinarily, this would've been fine, provided some kind of motor transport had been laid on for us between Cricklewood and St. Pancras (approx 6 miles), but as no one seemed to have any record of us after Bedford, we were left completely to our own devices! We didn't exist on paper therefore we didn't exist at all! In the end, we had to walk to Cricklewood Station, catch the next local service to Luton, board another local service from there back to Kings Cross Thameslink, before finally walking the short distance to St. Pancras. By this time, we were seriously in danger of missing the last train home, but amazingly, the station staff had been informed of our predicament and had held the train for us…some of them even cheered as we ran down the platform! Another time, a Bedford guard didn't turn up for duty and I was asked to remain with the train. I was working my rest day on this particular occasion, which meant I'd be on double time after midnight, but the thought of spending another thirteen hours (best case scenario), on top of the three I'd already worked, was just too much to bear…so I declined! Besides, I'd eaten all my snap on the journey down, which coincidently, broke the first rule of weekend ballast working…always save something for the twelfth hour!

The Elford Incident

Regardless of the myriad health and safety legislation that some people presume will automatically shield them from every mortal danger, accidents do happen, and the very nature of railway work constantly exposed its personnel to life threatening situations…whether they were always consciously aware of it or not! Sometimes though, these life threatening situations were entirely our own making…with a little bit of fate thrown in of course!

One Saturday night, I pulled out of Chadd' with perhaps the longest train I'd ever worked. It must've been nearly half a mile in length, and with a pair of 31s on the front, it looked a real monster! Just preparing it in the sidings meant I'd already walked a fair distance! The worksite was scheduled to be between Wichnor Junction and Tamworth Station, and we were required to wait in Elford Loop until the last passenger service had passed, at which point the possession would be granted. After safely clearing the main line, we waited in the loop as per instructions. Presently, the engineering supervisor appeared to discuss forthcoming train movements. Having already cleared it with the signalman, he asked if our train could set back towards the trap points at the entrance of the loop. (Trap points are a safety feature, situated to protect running lines should a train depart towards then from a loop or sidings without permission. The offending train would be deflected away from the running lines and derailed clear of the track.) It seemed a pointless move to me, and considering the length of our train, one that I wasn't particularly keen to undertake. However, apart from a sense of foreboding, I didn't have any definite objections as to why it couldn't be done, so after consulting with my driver, I walked back to check the available distance. Elford Loop is roughly a mile long (remember what I said about proper road learning!), so we had at least half a mile to play with. It was dark by this time, and I knew the length of our train would cause some difficulties, but the driver was watching for my signal, so using my hand lamp, I waved a green light across my body, which was the signal to set back slowly, at caution! Immediately after I'd given it, my lamp went dead. The battery was completely flat, and there was now no way of signalling the driver to stop! Unusually for a ballast crew, we were all still in our early twenties; the secondman was a renowned layabout, and the driver, without sounding nasty, wasn't overly bright, or adequately experienced with this kind of work. I don't know what he was thinking, but to my horror, he opened up fully and the train began setting back at an alarming rate! I waved my arms about like some demented windmill, but to no avail. I knew from past experience, that the secondman wouldn't even be looking anyway! Any normal person shunting at night, particularly under these circumstances, would've maintained a continuous signal with their hand lamp, primarily to reassure the driver that he was still proceeding as required. I would've done this, had I been able, but in the absence of any further signals, the driver should've stopped immediately…but this evidently wasn't happening!

There was only one way to stop the train now, and that was pull the vacuum pipe off the last wagon, but as they were passing me at roughly 10 mph, I would have to run like a maniac to catch up with the last one. I would've beaten any Olympic sprinter that night, as I raced down the ballast towards the end of the train. With a supreme effort, resulting largely from a mixture of adrenalin and pure terror, I climbed into the last wagon and reached over the side to pull the pipe off…but it was well out of my grasp! The trap points were looming dangerously close now, but the sheer exertion had left me completely breathless and I was at a loss what to do next. It's true I could've let the wagons run through the trap points, into the stop blocks and down the embankment, but I couldn't be sure, that on hitting the stop blocks, they wouldn't ride over each other, rear up in the air and foul the main line. The last express was imminent and there was absolutely no way of stopping it! Also, it suddenly dawned on me that I was riding in the last wagon, so even if they did all tumble down the bank and onto what looked like a concrete hard standing 20 feet below, I would be a certain fatality. Kicking the pipe off was now the only viable option.

In order to achieve this miracle, I had to climb over the side of the wagon and hang onto the left hand buffer sleeve, whereupon I could dangle my legs either side of the rail until my feet were dragging in the ballast. From this position, I was able to kick at the pipe with my right foot, all too aware of the burnished wagon wheel rapidly revolving between my legs, which would immediately slice me in half if I lost my grip! It took a few attempts, but my foot finally hit the pipe and it flew of its dummy connector. There was a noisy inrush of air as the vacuum was destroyed, and with much relief, I half jumped, half fell clear as the brakes began applying. I knew I'd taken a terrible risk, but I was a lot younger then, and youth coupled with agility had triumphed in the end! The severe and unexpected brake application must have virtually put the driver and secondman through the cab windscreen, but it was nothing less than they deserved! I was unable to worry about it, because at that moment, I was practically unconscious on the track, desperately trying to suck some air into my tortured lungs! The train came to a stand about six wagon lengths away from the trap points, seconds before the last express hurtled past on its way to Birmingham! The driver and secondman eventually came running up the track to try and ascertain what had happened, and if I hadn't been so spent, I would've knocked their silly heads together. Instead, I contented myself with the fact that at least one of them had a bloody nose from where it'd obviously connected with the windscreen! My train positioning turned out to be perfect for the engineering supervisor, who incidentally, remained completely oblivious to the terrible disaster I'd unwittingly set in motion, and then subsequently managed to avert! Unlike some "senior condom" who had just raised his ticket sales by five percent, no Silver Swift (The InterCity Achievement Award) was ever pinned on my chest! The incident was never reported, although I did have a few quiet words with my supposed crew afterwards…when I eventually got my breath back!

47331 passes Bennerley with a CE ballast train. Photo: P. Helme, circa 1993.

6. Cliffe Hill 1990

The Leicester & Burton Line (Part 1)

The Cliffe Hill job was the archetypal ballast working, and for most new trainmen at Derby, the first "mainline" route they learnt. All those weeks of rules and regulations suddenly began to make some sense and would undoubtedly be employed along this interesting, varied and challenging route. It was classic railway work and an excellent job to learn on because it could throw anything and everything at you…and often did, given enough time!

It was also an opportunity to work with, and get to know some of the old hand drivers who were regulars on the run. Characters like Driver Welsh for instance, who was a World War Two naval veteran and close to retirement. He reminded me of an aged version of Popeye, in both manner and speech, and was famous for referring to everyone as "brothel bred scum." He was also famous, or rather infamous, for his drivers' bag, the sole contents of which consisted of his lunch for the day, two very graphic adult magazines, and a large black marital aid! Initially, in my naivety, I thought he was a snake enthusiast of some sort, because almost everyone used to enquire about his black mamba! I don't know what the traction inspectors made of it, but it was an excellent prop for a bit of tomfoolery! On entering the mess room, he would usually label everyone as "brothel bred scum" before proceeding to fill his large teapot. Next he would sing a crude song or recite a dirty limerick whilst completing his timesheet, regardless of the fact that he hadn't actually done any work yet! It was then either a quick showing of the bag interior to a hushed and awestruck group, or a chance to use his other favourite catchphrase on some unsuspecting individual. "Do you want to see my war wound?" he'd ask, before parting his hair slightly to reveal a scar. "Someone smashed a bottle on my head in a brothel in Algeria in 1942!"

The purpose of the job was to fetch railway ballast for the CE department, for use in their track maintenance programmes on the eastern region, and there were two daily runs to Cliffe Hill. The first originated from Doncaster Wood Yard, and the second from Healey Mills. The trains were driver only operated by the eastern region men, for relief, usually at signal DY449. The signing on times for the Derby driver and trainman were 0601 and 1128 respectively. More often than not, it would be a Class 47 taking the strain, but once in a while, a Class 37 would put in an appearance. The train itself would be vacuum braked, normally consisting of a mixture of ZFV, ZEV, ZJV, and YGH ballast wagons. These code letters were the TOPS computer classifications, but most of the wagons in the CE fleet still retained their old telegraphic code names, which were all associated with the sea in some way. Therefore, the above wagons were better known to us as Dogfish, Catfish, Mermaid and Sealion. Sometimes a ZUV (Shark) plough brakevan would be included in the configuration as well. Once relieved, the eastern region driver would return home on the next passenger train, whilst the trainman would be informing the signalman that 7M74 was ready to depart.

Once the road had been given, a couple of notches on the power handle would set the train heading west out of Derby and through its environs of Peartree and Sunnyhill towards Stenson Junction. Willington Power Station would be passed on the left, then over North Stafford Junction, before reaching Clay Mills Level Crossing. This was a place you'd smell first before actually seeing, as there was a sewage farm situated right next to the crossing. There were also hot axle box detectors here, so if there was a problem with the train, now was the time to find out! If there happened to be an express following behind, the train could be switched onto the Down Goods at this point as well. Rounding the corner after Clay Mills, the digital clock on the Bass Brewery tower could be observed, its display alternating between the current time and temperature. If you were with one particular old hand driver, he would always remark on the time saying "We're a bit later/earlier than yesterday mate" so of course, your standard reply would always be "It's a bit colder/warmer today though." It was just one of those little rituals that had to be observed! The train would now be well and truly on the approach to Burton-upon-Trent, a place with its own distinctive smell, slightly more pleasant than the last one…one of beer brewing! After passing Wetmore Sidings, the train would proceed steadily through Platform 2, if it were still on the main line, or adjacent to it, if on the Down Goods. Either way, the route indicator signal would be lit and the train would be switched onto the Leicester & Burton Line at Leicester Junction, just after the end of the platform.

As the train snaked its way round towards Birmingham Curve Junction, the wagon wheels would always squeal terribly, no doubt in protest about being dragged around such a tight curve. I often expected a resident from nearby Cambridge or Oxford Street to complain, but living in the shadow of Drakelow Power Station, I suppose they were more than used to it. Once over the River Trent, the train would then pass through the well used Drakelow West and East Junctions. Drakelow B and C stations consumed a lot of coal, and there always seemed to be a train arriving, unloading or departing. In order to feed Drakelow's large appetite, the first half of the Leicester & Burton Line was dominated solely by coal production. The next point was Swadlincote Junction, which was a bit of a misnomer, as there was no junction there at the time. There used to a spur from the Up Goods to Cadley Hill Colliery, which had been taken out. This was replaced again in 1992, to serve Nadins opencast disposal point. After Swadlincote, the one and only tunnel on the route would be encountered next. At 623 yards, Gresley Tunnel wasn't particularly long, but a bit of an oddity in the fact that it (eventually) ended up with two speed limits. Going through on the Up Goods, the limit was 45 mph, but coming the other way on the Down Goods, it was only 10 mph. No one ever seemed to have a plausible explanation for this, although I think it's safe to assume that mining subsidence had a lot to do with it. One theory is that the Down Goods had been severely twisted due to this subsidence, and as wagons tend to sway at speed, the limit was considerably lowered to prevent them from coming into contact with the tunnel wall. Once this theory had been digested, I always found it a little unnerving to return with a loaded train through the tunnel. I used to wince involuntarily each time, expecting a wagon to connect with the brickwork and throw us off the track at any moment!

Visual evidence of the mining subsidence became apparent after Gresley Tunnel, as both tracks appeared alarmingly sunken and twisted, earning this spot the nickname of "The Big Dipper." Signalling control now passed from Derby PSB to Moira West Signal Box, and just after the train rattled through Moira West Junction, the box would be passed on the right. Opposite Moira Box was Rawdon Colliery and its associated sidings. Trains were still operating out of there, but during my tenure on the Cliffe Hill the colliery was eventually dismantled. Passing the last few active re-workings of Swains Park opencast, the track would then change to single line at Lounge Junction. Lounge Disposal Point would be on the left and signal control would change again to Mantle Lane Box. Once through Swannington Level Crossing, the train would enter the aptly named Coalville, with the depot on the right and Mantle Lane box opposite. This is where the trainman would normally alight, in order to stop the driver once the end of the train had cleared the shunt signal. The signalman would then set the road and the trainman would call the driver back into the reception sidings for a wagon examination.

Mantle Lane Signal Box, Jan 1992. Photo: Author.

Wagon examiners used cards to indicate any faults they found and would attach them to the offending vehicles accordingly. Predominantly green in colour, these cards allowed further travel but with certain restrictions imposed. For example, some were marked with a reduced speed, others stated that the wagon was not to be loaded, etc. For a serious fault however, a red card would be produced, which simply stated: Not To Go. This would be an unwelcome development, as the train crew would have to shunt the train and remove the crippled wagon. An old chap, who'd been given the nickname of "Red Card Jack" by some of the Derby drivers, often conducted the wagon examination. I'm not sure how he earned his name, because out of all the trains I worked through Coalville, I only ever had to knock out one cripple wagon. Driver Welsh was less than convinced though and would always remark, "Here comes Stop 'em Jack…brothel bred scum!" before breaking into a song about someone called Dirty Sally..!

Whilst the train was undergoing its examination, the crew could either go on a tea foraging mission to Coalville Mess Room, or perhaps partake of some footplate cuisine. One of the regular old hand drivers used to cook himself a full breakfast on the engine hotplate each morning. Instead of traction manuals, rule books and weekly notices, his driver's bag was full of eggs, bacon, sausages and the all-important frying pan! I believe Driver Welsh also ran his video empire from Coalville Mess Room, so he would often nip across to tantalize the lads with the latest releases, or collect any returns…although I doubt any of the titles would've appeared on a family viewing list! Once the wagon examination had been completed successfully, Jack would give the thumbs up and shout "Ok!" but Driver Welsh would pretend to be engrossed in one of his artistic magazines, so Jack would walk round to his side of the cab and shout again, but to no avail. In the end he'd have to climb up into the cab, "What's up driver, are you deaf?" he'd ask, allowing Driver Welsh to launch into another one of his favourite catchphrases.
"Deaf? You'd be deaf too, if you were on a battleship when a bomb came down the funnel and knocked all the crockery of the shelves!"

Once it was established that we were clear to proceed, the signalman would set the road and the train would draw out onto double track again, through Coalville Station Crossing with its distinctive signal box, and on towards Coalville Junction. Coalfields Farm would be passed

53

on the right, at the time, the last coal producing/loading facility of the route. The signalling responsibility would change again to Bardon Hill and the train would begin its climb towards the signal box and level crossing, passing Bardon Hill Sidings on the left. Finally, Cliffe Hill would be in sight and the train would draw up to No2 ground frame, situated near the B585 over bridge. The trainman would uncouple the engine, get the release for the ground frame from Bardon Hill box and set the road for the engine to run round. Quite often, the driver wouldn't bother changing ends, so the trainman would jump into the now leading cab, as the engine propelled down to No1 ground frame. This particular frame was electronic and at the push of a button, the trainman would set the road onto the wagons, call the driver back and re-couple the engine. During my first few runs as a novice trainman, I was always very wary about leaving the wagons on such a steep gradient whilst we ran round. According to the Rule Book, you were supposed to apply several wagon handbrakes, but as I was reliably informed, and as I eventually found myself through experience, the chances of vacuum braked wagons rolling away were extremely remote. Nevertheless, I often imagined the nightmare scenario of runaway wagons at Cliffe Hill and was always secretly relieved when the engine was re-coupled to the train. The whole train would then draw out past No1 frame, the trainman would push the button to set the road into Cliffe Hill (Tarmac) siding, before finally calling the driver back again. Once the train had set back into the siding, a series of lights controlled its movements during loading. The trainman would return control of the ground frame to the signalman, complete the necessary brake test and prepare a driver's slip, ready for the return journey. If he was a conscientious chap, he might also take the opportunity to examine each wagon after loading, just to ascertain there was no loose ballast anywhere. Once up to speed on the main line, these individual stones could become high velocity projectiles, which posed an obvious danger to passing trains. There was a spate of HSTs getting their carriage windows smashed whilst hurtling past ballast trains, so it eventually became a requirement to remove any ballast overspill.

Note the gradient! 47344 completes the run round manoeuvre at Cliffe Hill, Sep 1990. This photo was taken from the vantage point of No1 frame, just as the train is about to draw past, and set back into the siding for loading. Photo: Author.

Once loading had been completed, usually after two or three hours, the trainman would obtain permission to set the road onto the Down Goods, and the now designated E85 would be ready to depart. After a brief stop at Coalville to collect the TOPS list, and another wagon examination, it would be a steady run back to Birmingham Curve Junction. The train would often be held here to await a path back onto the Derby Birmingham Line. There is a recreation ground situated close to the track and whilst we were waiting one day, I noticed a lad with a dog standing on top of the slide. The dog was on a lead and watching us, but the lad was totally oblivious and was trying to encourage his pet down the slide. Eventually, the signalman pulled off and the driver gave a toot on the horn. Unfortunately, this startled the dog, which dragged its hapless owner face first down the slide. They both ended up in a heap at the bottom, but the lad managed to pick himself and give us several vigorous two fingered salutes before we disappeared...I didn't stop laughing until Clay Mills!

The only other delay may occur just before Derby. If the train happened to be running early, it would be routed into the passing loop at Sunnyhill, whilst the relieving eastern region driver was located. Otherwise, it was straight into Platform 1 for relief, and then back to 4 Shed to sign off duty. At 4 Shed, the TCS and roster clerk were seated behind a window and train crew would deposit their timesheets into a hatch underneath. On several occasions, Driver Welsh also deposited the fabled marital aid...much to the shock and annoyance of the roster clerk!

In general, the job was well structured and seemed to operate quite efficiently. However, its days were numbered, and by the end of 1990, Cliffe Hill was rendered obsolete and a new working devised into Stud Farm. Although Stud Farm was situated literally at the back of Cliffe Hill, it could only be accessed from the Leicester direction, so a group of us were sent to learn the second half of the line. Cliffe Hill wasn't the only place to be rendered obsolete in 1990, Coalville depot was closed in October of that year also. Its proud men were scattered by the four winds, although at least one of their number fetched up on our shores and was able to take a handful of Derby drivers and trainmen road learning. The marital aid was also retired, along with Driver Welsh!

7. Stud Farm 1991

The Leicester & Burton Line (Part 2)

No2 ground frame at Cliffe Hill marked the edge of the known world for me. I didn't sign any further and everything after that was an undiscovered country. After months of running round and returning home from this point, it seemed strange to contemplate venturing any further. In this seemingly lonely, desolate place, who'd want to go further? But what lay beyond Cliffe Hill...we were the Derby pioneers! During February 1991, a small group of drivers and trainmen were given two days road learning on Stud Farm. This basically involved taking a spare engine off the shed and travelling the length of the Leicester & Burton Line (approx 30 miles), concentrating primarily on the Leicester end and the movements in Stud Farm itself. On the first day we rattled up and down the line in a pair of 20s (20058/20087), then on the second day it was the turn of 47973...all regular Derby engines!

After Cliffe Hill No2 frame, the next point was Bagworth Junction, which was the access into Stud Farm, but only from the Leicester direction...unless of course you were light engine, in which case you could go behind the shunt signal, change ends, and drive in. At 565 feet, Bagworth Summit was the highest point on the line, and also where signalling control changed from Bardon Hill box to Leicester PSB. After which it was a fairly rapid single line descent down to Desford Level Crossing, past the golf course and through another level crossing at Kirby Muxloe, before heading into the more depressed area of Braunstone on the outskirts of Leicester. Once across Aylestone Viaduct, past Vic Berry's and the small power station at Saffron Lane, it was merely a case of awaiting the signalman's pleasure to cross you over the main lines at Knighton Junction, and into the passing loop. Once in the loop, it was either back to Derby via Burton, or via Leicester...the latter being the quickest! Waiting at Knighton allegedly had its compensations, as the cab was level with the bedroom windows of the nearby houses. According to legend, there was supposed to be a woman in the end house who always did aerobics in the nude! I never saw her and no one I worked with ever did, but it was always mentioned...and we always looked!

The basic structure of the Cliffe Hill diagram remained the same, only the timings and destination changed. The signing on times were now 0609 and 0954 and the first runs began in March. The Stud Farm facility was supposed to be a step forward, but I could never understand why it had been designed with single line access from one direction only, and why it could only accommodate one train at a time...but then again, I was just a lowly trainman! To compound these errors, the powers that be, in their wisdom, decided our two jobs would have to go via Burton...both on the outward and return journey! To put this in perspective, this meant plodding up to Cliffe Hill as normal, carrying on past Stud Farm and continuing all the way down to Knighton, where the engine would be run round, ready to drag the train all the way back up to Stud Farm! After loading, it would be back down to Knighton to run round, before traversing the Leicester & Burton Line in its entirety again, to finally end up at Derby for relief...quite a torturous 108 mile trip! Why we couldn't go via Leicester each way, I'll never know, although I seem to recall a familiar and often used phrase at the time; "pathing problems." Another problem was that there were at least two other jobs into Stud Farm besides ours, and as everything seemed to run hideously late most of the time, we often tended to clash. Arriving relatively trouble free at Stud Farm, albeit in a roundabout sort of way, didn't always guarantee immediate access. If there happened to be one of these jobs already loading, your train would have to set back into the refuge siding and wait its turn…a truly painful experience all round!

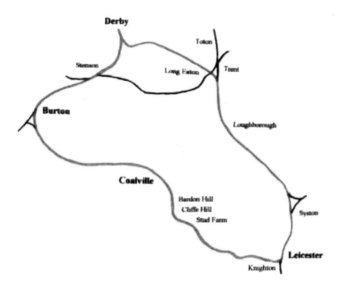

The Ballast Circuit. Approximately 73 miles round trip. Drawn by Author 2005.

The movements in Stud Farm were straightforward enough; the train would proceed over the weighbridge on slow speed and continue up the loading road. Once in clear, the engine would be run round and the wagons propelled back until the first one was positioned under the loader. It would then simply be a case of drawing forward to load each wagon, under the control of the bunker staff using a two-way radio. The resident "tapper" would carry out a wagon examination, and once loading had been completed, there would be a further wait for the train list to be printed, before proceeding slowly over the weighbridge once more and final departure in the Leicester direction. Waiting for the train list added insult to injury. Sometimes it could be forty minutes or more before TOPS Control decided to send it through, but for some unknown reason, the train was not allowed to depart without it! Why a manual train list and a driver's slip were not considered sufficient for the return journey, I never understood, but it was yet another example of inefficiency!

By my reckoning, only four trainmen ever signed Stud Farm initially…and I was one of them! I can't blame people for avoiding the job, it was a regular twelve hour shift, and that was only if it ran to some sort of schedule! After the carefree innocence of Cliffe Hill, this job came as a bit of a shock and could be quite soul-destroying if you weren't prepared for it. The best strategy was to accept that it was going to be a long day, set your stall out, and just think of the overtime! I regularly averaged a seventy hour week, with a personal best of ninety six hours in one week, although this was with a rest day and a Sunday worked as well!

47344 loading at Stud Farm, Jun 1991. Photo: R. King.

My other claim to fame was a fifteen hour day, due to our engine failing at Bagworth. The driver and I were on the 0609 job and had successfully loaded the train, run round at Knighton and were making good progress from Desford up to Bagworth. Once we hit the steep incline though, our weary Class 47 got slower and slower, eventually coming to a stand about half way up. No amount of coaxing could get it moving again, so I walked up to the signal phone at Bagworth and informed Bardon Hill of our predicament. The signalman told me that an assisting engine would arrive in the rear, obviously from Leicester depot I assumed. This sounded promising, as there was always a good spread of 47s, 56s and 58s to choose from…plenty of motive power to push our train up the bank! On hearing this, the signalman actually laughed "Oh no, you can't have any of those engines…they're a different sector to you!" Don't we all work for the same railway I wondered? "Besides, your assisting engine is coming from Wellingborough!" he added. So much for the different business sectors! The available engines at Leicester were most likely coal, parcels, or even construction livery, but because we were officially a departmental train, they couldn't be allowed to assist us…all because of a different colour scheme!

After informing my driver, I walked to the rear of our train, put down detonator protection and waited for the assisting engine. My all-enduring memory of the Leicester & Burton Line is that it always seemed permanently cold! The spot where we were stuck was particularly windswept and I was freezing. It was now beginning to get dark and there was still no sign of our assistance. I walked back to the engine to fetch my hand lamp and have a quick warm, before returning to my lonely vigil at the furthest detonator. After another hour of waiting, I walked all the way back up to Bagworth to contact the signalman again, only for him to tell me the engine had been delayed…as if I didn't know! Apart from occasional trips to the engine, I remained waiting at the furthest detonator. Eventually, far off in the darkness, I could hear a distant rumble of an engine. First it would seem quite close, then the sound would disappear altogether and I began to think I was imagining things, until finally the sound of an approaching engine was unmistakable.

After four hours, we were finally rescued by a single 31 (in B.R. blue livery!) from Wellingborough…what a way to run a railway! After checking its approach with my hand lamp, I climbed aboard. The deathly silence I'd grown accustomed to was suddenly punctuated with the shocking noise of my detonators exploding under its wheels, as we continued towards the rear of our train. After conferring with my driver and the signalman, we were ready for the big push and whistled up accordingly. The amp gauge in the 31 probably melted, but somehow this little engine managed to shove us up the bank and we were able to propel our wagons into the refuge siding at Stud Farm. I secured the wagons and coupled the two engines together for a brisk run down to Knighton, and an eventual weary arrival on Leicester shed. My driver and I managed to catch the next passenger train to Derby, but we didn't get off the hook that easily. The next day, after we'd had our required twelve hours rest, it was light engine to collect our wagons and complete the job!

It was obvious, even to us at ground level, that things couldn't continue the way they were. Train crews were beginning to abandon the job after eight hours, leaving the wagons in Knighton Old Sidings and returning to Derby light engine…and who could blame them? No matter how enthusiastic or dedicated you were, the timings were simply unworkable. By the end of July, the Stud Farm job was shelved as far as Derby men were concerned, and a new working devised into Bardon Hill.

8. Bardon Hill 1991-93

The Leicester & Burton Line (Part 3)

It must have been around 0500 on a fresh January morning, as I squeezed between the engine and first wagon at Knighton, attempting to disconnect the icy vacuum pipe and coupling. I had on about five layers of clothing, but it didn't make any difference, the cold still cut straight through me and we hadn't even set off up to Bagworth yet! Cold?..I don't think I'd ever been so cold in all my life! The "old hands" used to say that when you were on Bag'orth Summit, the next highest point as the crow flies was Siberia, and that's where the cold came from! Now being a veteran on the line, I was quite prepared to believe it!

I'll be honest and say I didn't care much for the Bardon Hill job. Its only saving grace was that we were finally operating on the route, as we should've done all along. The outward journey was now via Leicester, run round at Knighton, straight up the Leicester & Burton Line to Bardon Hill, where the trainman would use the ground frame and set the train back into the sidings. He would then uncouple the engine and Bardon's own shunter would collect the wagons and take them into the quarry to be loaded. After which, it was back to Derby via Burton…all very straightforward! The signing on times for the train crew were now 0335 and 0714 respectively. The 0714 job was tolerable, but I always found 0335 a punishing time to start work, especially in the depths of winter. It was also a notorious time for people not turning up, so if you happened to be 0005 spare, there was a good chance you'd be sent on the job. This was not a pleasant prospect when you'd been sat in the mess room over three hours and were expecting an early finish!

The journey to Leicester at that time in the morning always seemed grey and uneventful and there was little conversation to be had. Even if you had a decent driver for company, no one felt like talking. Besides, there was nothing to comment on, the rest of the world was still asleep and you so wished you could join them! It always felt cold running round at Knighton, regardless of the time of year. Once uncoupled, I tended to wait with the train whilst the engine proceeded to Wigston Junction, returning via the main line to be put back into the loop. There were a variety of ways the signalman at Leicester PSB could do this, and there seemed to be a different method every day. Even some of the very experienced drivers weren't sure of all the moves, so the trainman's knowledge became invaluable. It could be an odd experience advising a senior top-link driver how to run round at Knighton! Once the engine had been re-coupled, the trainman would walk to the rear of the train, fit a tail lamp to the last wagon, and perform a brake test. Whilst walking the length of the train, you would sometimes encounter a wall of heat, which was most unnatural considering the ambient temperature. This phenomenon immediately indicated that the wagon nearest to you was undoubtedly suffering from dragging brakes. After ascertaining its handbrake was fully off, the next step was to pull the vacuum release string and kick the brake blocks to ensure they'd been released properly.

Once accepted onto the Leicester & Burton Line, you were normally the first morning train to negotiate the single line through the rather dubious area of Braunstone, so it wasn't uncommon to come across the ubiquitous supermarket trolley placed strategically on the track…or even the odd washing machine, as was the case for one particular crew! On arrival at Bardon Hill Sidings, the trainman would alight near the ground frame whilst the train continued clear of the points. After ensuring all the necessary hand points were set for an empty road, he would then operate the frame and call the driver back into the sidings. It was important for the trainman to actually make a physical check of the hand points, as what often appeared to be an empty road, sometimes wasn't! Bardon Aggregates shared this siding with Prismo Bitumen and it wasn't uncommon to find wagons left foul. It was just one of those places where it was so easy to slip up, particularly during the early hours! Also, no matter where you stood, you could never see the end of the train as it set back into the sidings, so you were never quite sure what you were setting back onto...particularly as there was an internal vehicle crossing to consider as well!

A bleak Bardon Hill Ground Frame & Sidings, Feb 1992. Photo: Author.

My other dislike of the job was the interminable waiting around in the sidings. Once the shunter had coupled on and dragged the wagons away, there was nothing to do...there wasn't even any scenery to look at! At least at Cliffe Hill or Stud Farm, you were an active part of the loading process. You could see how many wagons had been loaded and how many were left, and more importantly, you could roughly gauge when you'd be heading home again, but there was none of this interaction at Bardon Hill. Two of Bardon's own men operated the shunter, but their brusque manner never really endeared them to me, especially during the bleak early hours! Once our engine had been uncoupled, the wagons were supposed to be their responsibility, but they always seemed reluctant to emerge from their engine for any great length of time. As our trains were all vacuum braked and their shunt engine was air only, they left it to the trainman to pull the vacuum release strings on every wagon, so they could just couple on and drag them away. If the train wasn't fully prepared when they decided to collect it, I often used to find that it had been interfered with on its return; perhaps a wagon handbrake applied somewhere, several instanter couplings changed to the long position, or the tail light missing...all rather petty and unnecessary! As our trains became longer, the internal vehicle crossing became fouled also. Local rules dictated that B.R. staff were not permitted to split the train in the sidings, so the lorry drivers would complain to the signalman, who would phone the local traffic manager, who would tell us to split the train, whom we in turn would inform that the wagons were not our responsibility in the sidings...and around it would go! As I said, all very unnecessary, simply because the wagons couldn't be dragged clear immediately on our arrival!

47352 awaits its train in Bardon Hill Sidings, Jul 1991. Photo: R. King.

As basic communication, common sense and courtesy often seemed in short supply, it was always a relief to depart Bardon Hill and head for home. The last remaining obstacle was still Sunnyhill Loop though, and the waiting time for both jobs seemed to have increased drastically. On average, it could be an hour or more before the signalman at Derby PSB allowed you into the station for relief. Sometimes you'd sit there so long that you'd begin to hallucinate. More than once, a driver has suddenly awoken from a half doze, flicked the controller from engine only to forward, thinking the trap points had gone over and that he was about to get the road! On one occasion, a trainman thought he was definitely hallucinating when he happened to casually glance out of the cab window and see a complete forearm and hand lying on the ballast! Expecting to see other parts of a tailor's dummy scattered around, and not succeeding, the grim realisation suddenly hit him. Just around the corner from Sunnyhill is Peartree Station, a notorious spot for vandalism…and suicides!

Stud Farm Revisited 1993-94
By the end of 1993, the job changed yet again…with a return to Stud Farm! There were still two jobs running, but for us, they no longer originated from Doncaster or Healey Mills. Our jobs were now both trip workings starting from Derby. The 93 trip (T93) had a signing on time of 0700 and was light engine off the shed to collect the empty train from either Chaddesden Sidings, or Sandiacre Ballast Sidings at Toton. The 91 trip (T91) was revived, and with a new signing on time of 0915, also had a similar diagram to T93. The vast majority of trains were collected from Sandiacre and departed via the high level goods line to Leicester. After which, it was the usual run round at Knighton and strenuous climb up to Stud Farm. With the job returning via Leicester and straight into Toton Centre via the high level, it only remained for the train crew to propel and secure the wagons in Sandiacre, before returning light engine to Derby, and a generally reasonable finish…the job had finally come full circle! It was the same for me too, the Cliffe Hill had been my first job as a new trainman, and now, in 1994, with redundancy inevitable, Stud Farm became my last!

9. The York Tanks

When you spent most of your time on the largely unglamorous local shunt and trip work, a run to York with a potentially dangerous cargo was quite an adventure…and brief elevation in status! I enjoyed working the York tanks for several reasons; for a start, it was a brakevan job and they were a real novelty for a modern day trainman! Once ensconced in your little home from home at the rear of the train, you were your own boss. You could stand out on the veranda in summer and watch the world go by, or cosy up to a nice hot stove in winter. For me, it was proper, traditional railway work…but work that was all too quickly disappearing!

Riding in a brakevan, as opposed to the cab of an engine, was a truly unique experience. Unique because when you are in an engine cab, everything is in front of you and ultimately heading your way, but in a brakevan, you see everything in review, or perhaps a more appropriate word is retrospectively. It's hard to explain fully, but for me, a deeper familiarity to a particular route would develop, purely from the raw motion of the brakevan. You felt closer to the track and therefore shared a greater connection to it, more so than in the cab. As many of the old hand guards (or Trainman G), could attest to, it was perfectly possible, even if blindfolded, to know exactly where you were on a route, just by the feel of the train on the track; different speeds and gradients, movement over junctions, noises the wheels made, even trackside smells, all gave a clear indication of your exact location…every bump and lurch meant something! All these sensations were obviously perceptible from the cab, but to a lesser degree I think. The brakevan added a unique atmosphere and the only way to recreate that up front would be to have a steam engine pulling the train! I also found the journey to York via the old road fascinating, which added to this feeling of nostalgia. There was much industry, past and present, to be observed along the way, all in perfect harmony with the railway. But most of the people and places had, or were about to be, consigned to the history books…and much of our way of life was destined to suffer the same fate too.

Designated 6E70 and headed by a Class 47, the train normally consisted of about 12 chlorine tanks, with a barrier wagon at each end and the inevitable brakevan bringing up the rear. The job originated from Bescot and its destination was the ICI plant at Wilton, situated beyond Tees Yard towards Redcar. The Derby driver and guard signed on at 1256, relieving the Bescot crew at Platform 1. As soon as the guard was aboard, it was important for him to take possession of the train list. This identified the hazardous material(s) being conveyed, the individual wagons, an emergency telephone number, and finally, the necessary signed authority for the train to proceed. The stove would already be glowing, regardless of the season, but a wise guard would wait until the train was under way before putting his mash can on to boil. Even so, during the course of any brakevan journey, a full can of water could be rapidly reduced to a thimble full…particularly with a rough driver! Once the signalman had given the road, the guard would show his green flag to the driver and await the inevitable lurch on departure! This of course, was the textbook method of departing a station, which didn't always correspond to real life, especially when a certain guard, renowned for his talkative ability, was paired with a driver whom, due to his intense dislike of overtime, was permanently in a rush to get home…

As the relieving Derby crew walked down the platform towards the train, the brakevan would be encountered first, so on arrival at the engine, the driver could safely assume that the guard was aboard, and had been for several minutes. Ordinarily this assumption would be correct, but on this day, as the aforementioned duo made their way down the platform, the guard espied the Station Master and proceeded to engage him in some lengthy discussion. The driver meanwhile, already in a hurry to get done, continued to the engine and climbed into the cab. Realising he'd been given the road, he immediately opened the power handle and got underway! The guard was still engrossed in his conversation, but on seeing the black exhaust plume issue from the distant engine, he suddenly realised he was meant to be elsewhere! Quickly bidding the startled Station Master farewell, he ran after the now rapidly departing brakevan, and literally threw his bag and himself onto the veranda. As the train disappeared over Derby North Junction, the Station Master was left scratching his head, no doubt pondering the manner of such men!

Northbound from Derby, the first tunnel on the route was Milford, situated between Duffield and Belper. You knew it was coming, but it still came as a shock to be suddenly plunged into complete darkness, save for the comforting glow of the stove. At 855 yards, it was long enough to be disorientating, so now was a good time to ascertain the exact whereabouts of your Bardic hand lamp! After Belper Station, the train might be turned in at Broadholme Loop to allow an express past, or a passenger service to either enter or exit the Matlock Branch, but with the picturesque Derbyshire countryside as a backdrop, there were worse places to be held. The open countryside also offered a brief interlude before encountering the next major tunnel at Clay Cross. At 1 mile, 24 yards, this was a real black hole, and whenever I travelled through it in a brakevan, I always wondered what it'd be like to get stuck in there…until one day it actually happened! On this particular occasion, the train was about halfway through when I became aware of the brakes being applied. This in itself wasn't unusual, particularly since Clay Cross Junction was the next point after clearing the tunnel, but as a rule, this job didn't encounter many red signals. For some strange reason, most signalmen were keen to pass us on as quickly as possible! My eyes hadn't quite adjusted to the darkness yet, but fortunately I'd kept my Bardic close at hand and shone it on the wall where the emergency air brake and gauge were situated. This was obviously no ordinary brake application, as the needle continued its rapid descent to zero and we finally came to a juddering halt! As there were no means of communication with the driver, it could've been an emergency application for all I knew, but from the evidence, I suspected that his foot had momentarily slipped off the DSD pedal. Nevertheless, this was serious because as we were carrying dangerous goods, the rules now dictated that I immediately apply a track circuit clip (a length of wire with a metal clip at each end) to the adjacent running line, and stop the job completely! When placed on each rail of the track, the clip acts like a wheel and axle combination of a train and causes a short circuit, giving the impression that that particular section is occupied, thus putting the signal in the rear to danger. I grabbed a clip and was just contemplating a dark and perilous trek down the tunnel with my detonators, when I heard the air building up again. It was fortunate that I hadn't yet alighted the brakevan because as soon as the gauge needle hit 72.5 psi, the train lurched clumsily off again! Apparently I had weighed up the situation correctly, but I think the driver removed a couple of years from my life expectancy that day!

At Clay Cross Junction, the train would be switched onto the Down Goods, passing the large coking plant at Avenue before crossing the London Midland/Eastern Region boundary at Horns Bridge. The plant at Avenue reinforces my earlier statement about trackside smells…with its thick, sulphurous atmosphere, there was little doubt that you were somewhere between Clay Cross and Chesterfield! The crooked church spire at Chesterfield also provided an unmistakeable landmark, as the train bypassed the station and continued on through Tapton Junction towards Barrow Hill. Lines of drab HAA coal hoppers filled the sidings here, sullenly awaiting their next MGR (merry go round) trip…a brief respite from their relentless journey of colliery to power station to colliery again! After a quick glimpse of the depot roundhouse, the train would continue past Renishaw Park Colliery and Orgreave Coking Plant before encountering Treeton Junction. On rare occasions the train could be diverted here, to pass through the vast, but now largely derelict Tinsley Yard. However, as a special order was required beforehand to divert any dangerous goods trains, there were generally few surprises to be had. The main industry would then briefly switch from coal to steel, as the train progressed through Rotherham Masborough and the complicated looking Aldwarke Junction, before coal returned with a vengeance. Manvers, Goldthorpe, Hickleton, Frickley, and South Kirby collieries lay between four small provincial stations, after which came the rather grim looking platforms of Pontefract Baghill. Ferrybridge Power Station would now be in sight, and once in the shadow of the cooling towers, the guard would usually acknowledge a wave from the signalman there, before the train rumbled over the River Aire and immediately into Brotherton Tunnel towards Milford Junction. Occasionally you'd catch a glimpse of the large coal barges on the river, carrying out much the same duties as the MGR trains, but perhaps in a more majestic manner!

After Milford Junction came Sherburn-in-Elmet, Church Fenton and Ulleskelf stations, or as one old hand guard used to refer to them: German in a helmet, Shane Fenton and ukulele! Industry now gave way to more open country once again, and on a nice clear flying day, several Jet Provost aircraft could be spotted in front of the hangers at RAF Church Fenton. Around this point the track began to sweep round in a lengthy curve, so it was possible to look back from the veranda and see another train following behind in the next but one section. This could be a little unnerving, especially when you spent most of your time up front in a cab, never really considering what was happening behind…but you had to assume the signalman knew what he was doing! After Ulleskelf came Colton Junction with its high-speed crossover, where a HST could switch from one main line to another without slowing. The train was now well on the approach to York, and after passing the largely empty Dringhouses and Holgate sidings, the unmistakable canopied station would be in sight, with the Minster in the background. To bypass the station, the train would be signalled into York Yard South, where a Thornaby crew would relieve the Derby driver and guard. The Derby men would then make their way across the tracks to the station, in order to catch the next passenger train home…or back on the cushions as it was sometimes referred to! With the crew arriving back in Derby around 2000, it was a satisfactory conclusion to an efficiently run job…before the impending, but inevitable changes.

Return Workings
Although Derby didn't really play a part in the return working of the tanks, there were often instances when it was diverted and we were thus called upon to conduct the Bescot men via Leicester and Nuneaton…a laborious, roundabout journey to be sure! The timings for this particular trip weren't too appealing either, as the Derby crew were required to sign on duty at 0212! No matter how often I worked these unnatural hours, I never got used to them. Walking into the mess room at that time in the morning felt more like a dream than reality. Spare men would view you cautiously with half open eyes. The odd grunt of acknowledgement, or enquiry as to your destination might be forthcoming, but once it had been established that you were neither threat nor benefit to them, they would return to their partially comatose state!

The job would eventually arrive in the station, and after greeting our respective Bescot counterparts, I would give a green signal from the brakevan indicating that we were clear to depart. First it would be the usual uneventful trip out to Leicester, passing the all too familiar

Knighton Loop, then the train would virtually turn back on itself at Wigston Junction and head down the South Leicester Line. At most times, I considered this to be a largely uninteresting stretch of track, but at this time of the morning, it was especially dark and nondescript. Apart from Croft sidings situated between Narborough and Hinckley, things didn't really become exciting until we reached Nuneaton Midland Junction. At this point, we were often routed high level over Nuneaton Station. There would be a brief sensation of mid air flight as it passed beneath us, before encountering the box at Abbey Junction, where the signalman was keeping his lonely vigil. After Nuneaton came Arley Tunnel, but its approaches were naturally gloomy, even during the day, so only the increased draught and change in air pressure indicated that you were actually passing through it. This was the difference between day and night travel in a brakevan. During the dark hours, the senses were dulled and the monotonous motion was sometimes disorientating. With every unexpected bump or lurch, the Bescot man would glance in my direction and I would try to look confident that I knew exactly where we were on such a dark, indistinguishable track. Our roles would be reversed however, once we encountered the vast expense of Sutton Park. After the tunnel, Daw Mill Colliery and sidings would be passed next, before the train emerged at Water Orton. From here, it was turned across to Sutton Park and Walsall.

After working its way round Pleck Junction, the train would finally enter Bescot and the Derby crew would alight at the engine holding sidings. There were often several rows of idling Class 31s stabled here, all belching out thick, choking diesel fumes. After emerging from the brakevan, bleary-eyed and experiencing symptoms akin to severe jet lag, this sweet, sickly cloud really completed the wretchedness of your condition! The first passenger train arrived at Bescot Stadium around 0600, so there would perhaps be time for a cuppa before heading to Birmingham New Street, and the interminable journey home. There was one small bonus from these trips...I eventually added Bescot to my road card!

10. On The Denby

Job Number 422 / Rostered 8hrs 55mins

"Who's on the Denby then?"
This was the question usually echoing around 4 Shed Mess Room around 1215 every weekday. I think it was asked more out of panic than actual interest, because if someone didn't show up for it between now and 1230, things didn't look too promising for anyone unfortunate enough to be sitting spare, and who signed the road! It was a relief then, when the designated crew did show up. People expecting to be landed with the job could now relax and make fun of the chosen three who would have to tackle the branch once again.

The Denby arrives! Photo: P. Helme, circa 1987.

I remember "The Denby" being largely unpopular amongst the Derby Trainmen, but to a couple of us at 4 Shed, it was what working on the railway was all about. Within its diagram, you had all the essential elements of proper railway work. People went to great lengths to avoid it, which always seemed strange to me, as they missed out on the enormous entertainment value the branch had to offer. What true railwayman could resist collecting a token and running 36 empty HAA wagons and two brakevans up a five mile single line branch, negotiate no less than 7 trainman operated crossings, perform a unique shunting operation, and then return with nearly 2,000 tonnes of power station coal. To further complicate matters, standing orders required that all this had to be accomplished before darkness, fog or falling snow. Not always an easy task when signing on duty at 1222 during the winter months…especially if the job was already running late! Of course, traversing the branch was only one part of the job. The train would then have to proceed to Willington Power Station to unload, before returning to Toton via the Stenson Branch. The empties would be put onto the Old Bank Sidings and the engines (usually a pair of 20s), onto the fuel line. Even then, it wasn't over for the Derby men, as it was often a mad dash for the 1925 staff mini-bus to Long Eaton Station, to catch the next train back to Derby…that's if you were running to schedule! Perhaps this is why the job was never well received..?!

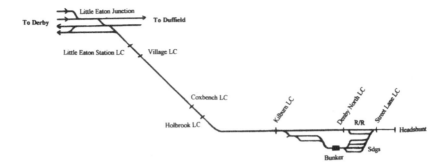

Track Diagram of the Denby Branch (pre 1991). Drawn by Author.

As the crew were signing on, the first of two questions was always asked of the TCS; "Is it running?" A nod of the head, often accompanied by a sadistic grin, would then immediately elicit the second question; "Where is it?" As the train originated from Toton, it was unusual for there to be any major delays, so after forty minutes or so, the TCS would phone through to the mess room to inform the crew that it was waiting for them on the Down Goods. Whilst the driver and secondman had to trudge all the way along Platform 6 to the north end of Derby Station for the engine, the guard was able to climb into the brakevan straight away, as it sat almost on the foot crossing near the mess room. On relieving the Toton men, the secondman and guard would ensure they had obtained a two-way radio and a crossing gate key apiece, a radio check would then be made and the signalman informed that they were ready for the off.

On one occasion, we had to collect the train from St Mary's reception, which was roughly half a mile down the line, but as Big Bill, our driver was of the more portly persuasion and not keen to walk too far, we managed to scrounge a lift from someone signing off duty. We were dropped in an industrial estate close to the track and had to scramble up an embankment to the train. Big Bill however, was unable to negotiate this obstacle, so whilst I endeavoured to pull him up, our secondman had his shoulder firmly wedged against his rear and was rather ungracefully shoving him up…I think it was the only time where an actual driver required banking assistance! *(An engine that pushed or pulled a train up a steep gradient was called a banker, hence banking assistance.)*

Once in the brakevan, the guard would first check the status of the fire, then a quick glance to ensure the necessary safety equipment was aboard, and maybe even a read of the latest graffiti whilst waiting on the signalman…had anyone new made the Denby Hall of Fame? Membership was quite exclusive; you had to knock a gate down to qualify! (That being the case, I think I ended up becoming slightly over qualified!) If the driver was in a good mood, he might warn the guard that they were about to depart by means of the radio. Nevertheless, the guard would soon hear the unmistakable, and awful, metallic clang of the couplings as they stretched out between the wagons, starting from the engine and building up to a violent crescendo along the length of the train. BANG! The brakevan would immediately be yanked from a standstill to about 15 mph and anything not held securely in place would fly into the air. Essential tea making equipment, such as the mash can and mugs, previously benign objects, would suddenly become hostile projectiles!

It was always fun to have someone uninitiated in the ways of the brakevan, as they would be invited to sit down with a generous cup of tea, perhaps even begin to prepare a roll-up, only to wonder what this terrible clanking noise was rapidly heading their way, and why the other person was firmly wedged in a corner. The moment of realisation would eventually dawn, but it was always too late! The tea would be slopped, the tobacco would be flung over the shoulder and the head would involuntarily make contact with the wooden panel wall…many a curse was relayed to the driver via the radio after a rough departure!

Life in the Brakevan – A home from home? Photo: Author, Mar 1992.

On departure from Derby, the train would continue along the Down Goods for approximately three miles before reaching Little Eaton Junction, and the start of the Denby Branch proper. The train could be held here, sometimes for an indeterminate length of time, as Toton men often ran a morning job and may still be occupying the branch. At peak efficiency with the rapid loader in operation, three trains per day were run up the branch, the first two operated by Toton men. Also, the train would have to await a path across the main lines, so any Derby man departing north on a passenger service would recognise the job with its unique configuration of a brakevan at each end, realise it was being held for him, and ultimately whistle "Arseholes" as he shot past!

Eventually permission would be given to proceed onto the branch, where the first set of gates would be encountered at Little Eaton Station Crossing. More importantly, this is where the token had to be collected and given to the driver; the first reason being, to give the driver protection to travel along the single line branch, and the second reason being, to unlock the ground frame at Kilburn…quite essential for the return journey! There were stories of a secondman who once forgot to collect the token, a serious error in itself, but even worse when he found he was unable to operate the ground frame! Fortunately, there is an excellent bus service, which runs virtually parallel to the branch, and so, he was dispatched by a rather annoyed driver to retrieve the vital token.

Little Eaton Station Crossing, Feb 1992. Photo: Author.

Once the token was on board and the secondman had opened the gates, the train could proceed through towards the next set at Little Eaton Village Crossing. There was barely a train length between these two crossings, so at this point, the rear of the train would be still be foul at Station Crossing. You could almost read the minds of the waiting motorists as the guard made his way up to the gates. The train has stopped; the guard is walking up…what's wrong? Eventually the secondman would open the gates at Village; I say eventually because these gates had been hit so many times that they would only open in a certain order! The train could then continue through, only to be stopped almost immediately whilst the guard closed Station Crossing. The trick for the guard now of course, was to accurately judge when to stop the train using the radio. If insufficient distance had been left between the rear of the train and the now closed gate, there may be enough slack in each wagon coupling for the train to set back by a couple of wagon lengths. The result being one red-faced guard, a few worried motorists and some freshly produced firewood!

Once the guard had secured Village Crossing, the train would then have a reasonable run to the former station at Coxbench, and its two pairs of gates. Two roads merged into one at this point, and both on practically blind bends. Although the road wasn't generally fast or busy, it wasn't uncommon to hear a squeal of brakes from an unsuspecting motorist suddenly encountering a gate across his path! Once through Coxbench, the train would proceed around the corner to Holbrook Crossing. There would be just enough clearance for the guard to secure Coxbench gates, before the secondman opened Holbrook, thus minimising the delay to traffic. Once Holbrook Crossing had been successfully negotiated, it would be a nice straight run for a mile, then under the A38 road bridge, before rounding the corner for the approach to Kilburn Crossing.

The Author gives a quick "thumbs up" as Holbrook is safely accomplished...next stop Kilburn! Photo: J. Riley, Mar 1992.

The two pairs of gates at Kilburn spanned a busy road and were possibly the most daunting on the route. A degree of patience was required to wait for a suitable break in the traffic before swinging them out! On one occasion, a new trainman learning the job hadn't reckoned with the speed of the traffic. He swung one of the gates out, causing a car to brake violently. The car managed to stop but another one ran straight up the back of it! The train continued through regardless and when I arrived on the scene, it had developed into a three car pile up...I'd never seen so much devastation! Fortunately no one had been hurt, so whistling innocently to myself, I quickly secured the gates and caught up with the rapidly departing brakevan!

The train would continue past the bunker and up through Denby North Crossing, passing the loaded wagons for the return journey. Once in the run round loop, the guard would uncouple the rear brakevan. The train would then proceed over Street Lane Crossing and into the head shunt, until the last wagon had cleared the sidings points. The guard would pull the hand points and call the train back, dropping the first three wagon handbrakes. Once the first road of the sidings had been filled, the bunker operative would uncouple, the guard would send the train forward, set the points for the next road and call the train back again. The wagons would normally be accommodated in the sidings within two or three of these movements. Street Lane Crossing would be secured, the guard would uncouple the engine(s) with the remaining brakevan, set the points and propel the brake into the run round loop to couple up with the other one. The engine would run round the brakevans, and once re-coupled, draw them both back through Denby North, to a point approximately fifty metres away from Kilburn gates, where the rear brakevan would be uncoupled. The engine and remaining brakevan would continue forward through Kilburn gates again, until clear of the ground frame, where the secondman would change the points and set them back onto the fully loaded train.

Preparing the train near Kilburn Crossing. Photo: P. Helme, circa 1987.

Kilburn Ground Frame and gates. Note the protrusion at the base of the levers (right), where the token would be inserted to unlock the frame. Photo: Author, Feb 1992.

If the guard was thinking ahead, he would bank the fire in his original brakevan (the one now behind the engine), and put a can of water on the boil. This would be his residence once more after running round at Willington Power Station. Also, a quick trip to the nearby shop would be in order, for a pasty to warm on the stove…and the usual pork pie for Big Bill! After examining the loaded wagons, calculating the driver's slip, and performing a brake test, the train would be ready for departure….and this is where the fun would begin!

Once the rear of the train had cleared Kilburn gates and the secondman had reset the ground frame, the guard was required to roll his brakevan onto the back of the train! It sounds easy, but it took quite a bit of skill to judge exactly. There was little room for error, as the results could be extremely embarrassing, particularly with several motorists for an audience. The basic theory was for the guard to release the handbrake just enough to get the van rolling, thus allowing the gradient to take over, whilst continuing to gently rub the brakes. The van would then trundle merrily over Kilburn crossing, to arrive at the rear of the train totally under control and ready to couple up?! I've witnessed both extremes of this manoeuvre, ranging from the nervous guard who releases the handbrake, only to re-apply it too soon and come to a dead stand on the crossing, to the deranged guard who releases the handbrake with total abandon, only to hurtle over the crossing, hit the buffers of the last wagon and be bounced back over the crossing…much to the amusement of the waiting motorists! In each case, with not quite enough gradient to get the brakevan rolling again, and too embarrassed to ask the driver to set back a little, you wouldn't think someone could push a 21 ton brakevan, but it was done on a few occasions! Once re-coupled, the secondman would retrieve the token from the ground frame and help the guard secure Kilburn gates, before returning to the engine.

Revised Workings

1991 saw the introduction of a rapid loader, making the whole operation a lot more efficient by rendering Street Lane Crossing, the sidings, and all the intensive shunting obsolete. On arrival at Denby, the engine (now usually a Class 56) would be set on slow speed and the empty wagons simply drawn through the rapid loader, under instruction from the bunker operative. The secondman would still open Denby North gates, but only at the last minute, as the train made its snail-like progress towards Street Lane and the end of the line. When opened, Denby North gates obstructed a quiet backwater lane, which served barely a handful of houses. There were perhaps four cars up and down all day, but as soon as the secondman opened the gates, one would suddenly appear, pushing to get across! It was the scene of several heated arguments, as one resident motorist in particular just couldn't understand why he wasn't allowed to cross in front of the train, as it continued its slow, but nevertheless relentless plod barely a car length away from him! Whilst languishing in the brakevan, the guard would probably use this time to prepare a driver's slip and put the all-important can of water on the boil, before transferring his belongings into the brakevan nearest the engine…if not already summoned to participate in an argument at Denby North that is! Whilst walking up, he would be able to give the wagons a cursory examination, as the bunker staff had a tendency to grossly overfill them!

Slow speed towards Denby North. Note the generously filled wagons! Photo: J. Riley, Jan 92.

Once loading had been completed, the guard would set the hand points and ride in the rear brakevan whilst the train set back through the rapid loader onto the adjacent road. Although the thrill of rolling the brakevan onto the train was no more, this manoeuvre sometimes had its moments. Two thousand tonnes could be a tricky load to handle downhill, especially on wet rail. With a foot crossing and then the trap points looming, it was a sensible guard who had one hand on the emergency brake and one foot on the step board ready to "bail out", particularly if the train was showing no sign of slowing down, or even worse…beginning to slide! Once in clear, the engine would be run round, ready for departure.

6D50 ready to depart, Jan 1992. Photo: Author.

The revised workings brought a new signing on time of 1147 for the Derby men. Then a strange practice of having assisting trainmen was introduced towards the end of 1992. From successfully operating the branch with just the driver, secondman and guard, there were suddenly two additional trainmen to assist with the gates. This was supposed to improve health and safety, and having more people was supposed to mean fewer accidents…but on this particular job, the results were often quite the opposite! As none of the gates had lights on them, or any sort of advanced warning, the reasons for not using the branch during darkness, fog, or falling snow were quite understandable. However, it was rare for the job to arrive at Derby so late that it couldn't be run up the branch in the daylight, but if, on arrival at Denby, conditions had deteriorated to a point where the train could not return, it would be left there until the following day and the crew would return light engine…an early finish!

On one occasion, the fog did descend on the approach to Denby, and an unfortunate trainman had an unexpected appointment with the resident nurse! The gates would be opened for the train and often just secured with a chain. However, a strange phenomenon would sometimes occur on the Denby Branch, whereby a gate would somehow release itself and fold in towards the train under its own weight. This happened just as the rear brakevan was about to clear Kilburn gates; the secondman was one side, the assisting trainman was the other, and the guard was on the brakevan…so far, so good! Unfortunately, the guard, thinking he was almost clear, had decided to stand on the stepboards, not expecting a gate to swing out of the gloom and clip his knees! His scream tailed off into the fog, as the train cleared the gates. The two trainmen, thinking they'd seriously injured him, caught up with the brakevan and tentatively peeked in the door. They were greeted by the sight of the guard, handkerchief in one hand, cigarette in the other, sitting with his trousers rolled up, exposing two rather skinned knees! If he'd knotted the handkerchief and put it on his head, he'd be perfect for Skegness beach! The trainmen had to quickly close the door to stifle a laugh, before entering seriously. The first words uttered by the guard proved he was okay, "I'm claiming my rest day!" It was suggested that he visit the nurse, so he hobbled off in the direction of the bunker. A short while later, another fog-piercing scream was heard, as the nurse liberally applied iodine to his raw knees. All in all, not a happy day for him!

The same guard always wore the double-breasted uniform jacket, which had a pen pocket on the inside. After securing Kilburn gates once, he inadvertently put the padlock key into this pocket. The pocket obviously had the same dimensions as a pen, but unfortunately his hand didn't, so it was impossible to retrieve the key. The waiting motorists looked on in amazement as he spun around, rather like a dog chasing its tail, his two fingers jammed into this pocket trying to reach the key. The nurse very nearly accosted him again, as she considered it to be a serious affliction of some sort…the only cure being another good dose of iodine!

6D50 powers away from Kilburn, Jan 1992. Photo: J. Riley.

The Denby phenomenon manifested itself for me one wet, grey December afternoon in 1991, as we made our way back down the branch. I was the guard on this particular occasion and was residing in the brakevan, attempting to keep dry between crossings. The train was halfway through Village Crossing when I decided to stick my head out to check our progress. I thought I was imagining things at first, but it suddenly dawned on me that the right hand gate wasn't secured properly. It flapped casually back and forth, almost mockingly, as each wagon past. I was silently urging the train to speed up so we'd get through before it came into contact with one of them...but it was not to be! I watched helplessly as the gate finally connected with a passing wagon. There was a terrible splintering of wood as it reared up and snapped in half like a twig! I duly jumped off the brakevan as it cleared the crossing, trying not to look at the rather white faced motorist who was at the front of the queue. He sat looking at me open mouthed, as I removed the debris from the road and his car bonnet.
"It saves me having to open them for you doesn't it!" I said cheerily, before retreating to the brakevan to contemplate yet another report form. There was a small bonus to be had from this mishap...there was no shortage of wood for the brakevan stove for a while!

You'd think there'd be plenty of fuel for the stove on a coal train, but power station coal is extremely fine and completely useless on a normal fire. You also had to make sure the brakevan door nearest the last wagon was closed, particularly on a hot, summer day, as once up to speed on the goods line, the forward motion of the train would funnel all the fine particles in your direction. You could hear them hitting the Perspex windows like rain, permeating everything.

EAST MIDLANDS (PASSENGER)

To : *Trainman T. Helme*
4 SHED

From : Area Manager
East Midlands (Passenger)
Traffic Office   Room 21
Wyvern House   Derby

Ref : *TQC/05/12/N/01/PB.*

Ext : 056 3342   FAX : 056 3158

Date : *10 - 12 - 91*

~~TRAIN DELAY~~ / INCIDENT CONCERNING *6D50 Empties Willington to Derby.*

ON *THURSDAY 5 - 12* 199/_

It has been reported that this train *Knocked a Gate off its hinges on the Denby branch.*

To enable investigations to be completed, it is necessary for me to obtain ~~full~~ / further details and I shall be grateful if you will

X a/   prepare a report

~~b/~~   ~~complete the attached form~~

and send it to me at the address shown at the head of this letter.

It is helpful if you quote my reference.

Your assistance will be appreciated. Thank you.

Once off the branch, the approach to Derby could often be entertaining, particularly if there were assisting trainmen aboard. They were now surplus to requirements and would be anxious to disappear at the earliest opportunity, passing on their timesheets, to be completed and handed in by the remaining crew. We were often routed through Platform 2, obviously non-stop, so anyone "bailing out" from the engine would stand ready in the doorway, whilst the driver slowed and checked the windows of Wyvern House for any management (imagined or otherwise), who happened to be looking out. Once the all clear had been given, departing train crew would develop a sort of clockwork style run/walk, as they exchanged a moving train for a stationery platform! If the same crew was booked on the job all week, arrangements would be made so that everyone had an early day at least once…provided the people remaining with the job actually had sufficient road knowledge! When Class 56s became the regular traction on the job, some Derby drivers weren't familiar with the engine, and so required a conductor driver to ride with them for a period of time. This was the scenario one particular day, as we rolled down Platform 2. It must have been a Friday because everybody wanted an early finish! The assisting trainman quickly departed, closely followed by the driver, leaving myself as secondman and the conductor driver at the controls. I suppose this would've been okay, except that it transpired that the conductor driver didn't have road knowledge of Willington Power Station, or the Stenson Branch! Everyone had been in such a rush to leave, that this *small* matter had been overlooked! I consoled the now worried conductor driver with the fact that I knew the route as well as anyone and would talk him through it as we progressed. Even though it was against all the rules, he requested that I drive instead, so I took over from Derby and we completed the job without incident.

Approximately four miles westbound from Derby, the train would arrive at Stenson Junction, where it would be routed into Willington Power Station. Once the engine had been run round again, the train would proceed through the bunker on slow speed to unload. As the wagons were drawn through, their doors would be opened automatically, dropping the coal onto a belt beneath, where it would usually be conveyed to a large storage pile. The guard would change brakevans for the last time, no doubt glad there was a can of boiling water and a nice warm pasty waiting for him, particularly if it was a dark winter evening. Although the fire gave some illumination, I often took a candle as well, making the brakevan almost a home from home, ready for the journey up the Stenson Branch to Toton.

Late afternoon arrival at Willington Power Station, Nov 1990. Photo: R. King.

Unloading at Willington Power Station, Apr 1992. Photo: Author.

It's approximately thirteen miles from Stenson Junction to Sheet Stores Junction via the branch, passing Castle Donnington Power Station (now demolished), and through Back Lane Crossing, before eventually passing under the M1, over the River Trent, and rounding the corner for Lock Lane Signal Box. One dark November night, it was my turn for an early finish and through prior arrangement with the secondman, it was decided that I would alight at Sheet Stores Junction, where it was usual for the train to be held. This was a convenient location for me to get to Long Eaton Station, and as I had an assisting trainman riding in the brakevan with me, I assumed everything would be okay and I could slip away into the darkness. Unfortunately I didn't take into account a very observant signalman at Lock Lane, who reported to control that the guard had absconded...yet another report to fill in!

Once through Sheet Stores Junction towards Trent East Junction, the train would pass Trent PSB and on towards Toton. The train would continue through Toton Centre and past Stapleford & Sandiacre Signal Box, right up towards Stanton Gate, before propelling the empty wagons onto the Old Bank. The engines would be uncoupled, to eventually arrive on the depot fuel line. The crew would then check in with the TCS, hand in the radios and keys, and either have a cuppa if they were on schedule, or make a mad dash for the staff mini-bus to Long Eaton Station and the next train to Derby...ready to do it all again the next day!

An occasional turf war was fought during the latter days, with Toton men working our 1147 job straight through, instead of getting relief at Derby. This continued sporadically, until we did finally lose the job to them.

11. Washwood Heath

There was never any mistaking the Washwood Heath job! Two Class 37s hauling 23 heavily laden RMC aggregate wagons, each in their distinctive orange and cream livery. Weighing in at around 2,500 tonnes, it was rivalled only in size and motive power by the Corby/Lakenby steel coil train. It certainly made an impressive sight as it snaked its way into Derby along the goods line. The train originated from Peak Forest and was operated by a Buxton driver, who would be relieved at DY449 by a full Derby crew. Signing on at 1453 (latterly 1433), the Derby men would then work the train to its discharge point at Washwood Heath, near Saltley. If the Cliffe Hill job was the first one to be learnt by a new trainman on the morning shift, then the Washwood Heath usually became the second one when he switched to afternoons. Both were regular runners and provided an excellent grounding for the novice trainman.

As the drivers exchanged places, the secondman would phone the signalman to get the road, whilst the guard would be deciding which cab to ride in! Officially he was supposed to ride in the rear cab of the lead engine, but I always favoured the lead cab of the second engine…as this way, I'd be facing in the direction of travel and could at least enjoy a bit of the view! I always found it quite thrilling to work the Washwood Heath, either as guard or secondman. It seemed such an exciting and high profile job, not to mention the responsibility that came with it. Although it was really just another aggregate train, having double-headed 37s was the real attraction for enthusiastic trainmen, and everyone took notice when you got under way! As the job was booked to travel at 60 mph, we were nearly always given a good run by the signalman. Quite often when I got on the phone they'd say, "If you get underway quick, I'll let you go in front of the express." So you'd tell your driver and off we'd go. Unfortunately, on one occasion, just as we were departing Derby, the driver's foot slipped off the DSD pedal and we came to a dead stand on London Road Junction! With a train this size, it took a while to blow the brakes off again, so the driver asked me to phone the signalman and tell him we'd come to a stand. As we were right next to the PSB, and had been blocking a main junction for nearly five minutes, he was no doubt fully aware of our situation and very likely doing a jig in front of his console at that very moment!

Once under London Road Bridge and around the slight curve towards Peartree Station, we'd sometimes encounter kids "playing chicken" on the tracks, particularly during the school holidays. As we rounded the corner one afternoon, there were suddenly about three of them stood in our path! Having only just departed Derby, we were still building up speed, but there was simply no way of stopping in time if one of them happened to stumble! I was the secondman on this occasion and gave them plenty of horn! Several blasts from such a formidable looking train was enough to make them think twice, and fortunately they moved in plenty of time. The next day as we warily rounded the corner, the sun was shinning directly on the rails causing a glare, but there was what looked to be a figure crouching or lying prone on the track! Again I gave plenty of horn, but this time there was no movement! Perhaps some kid had fallen over and knocked himself unconscious? There was a sudden sick feeling in the pit of my stomach, that no matter what anyone did, there was just no way of stopping. The terrible realisation that we were going to hit someone was bad enough, but the fact that we were absolutely powerless to do anything about it seemed much worse! The driver was just about to apply the emergency brake and hope for the best, when we both realised what it was…the prone figure turned out to be a black bin liner full of rubbish placed strategically between the rails! In the next second, we hammered over it on our way to Burton, but it took a while longer for the sick feeling to go away.

As the train approached Burton, the permanent 50 mph speed restriction before the station would set off the AWS horn, which the driver would then cancel before reducing speed accordingly. After the last wagon had cleared station limits, he could then open up again between Branston and Wichnor junctions, providing the train wasn't being turned into Elford Loop of course! Once through Tamworth and Wilnecote stations, the train would then rattle through Kingsbury Branch Junction, passing the oil terminal and scrap sidings on the left. After Kingsbury Branch came Kingsbury Junction itself, where depending on the mood of the signalman (now Saltley PSB), the train could be routed from the main line and onto the slow line towards Whitacre Junction. This four mile avoiding route sent the train round past Hams Hall Power Station and Coleshill Sidings, to eventually rejoin the main line at Water Orton Station. After which, it would be turned onto the Down Goods at Castle Bromwich Junction, to continue past Fort Dunlop and through the gloom of Bromford Bridge towards Washwood Heath. Finally, the train would be turned onto the RMC siding at Washwood Heath East Junction, coming to a stand just before the hopper house.

The guard's view from the cab of 37687, somewhere near Tamworth. Photo: R. King, Aug 90.

As one driver used to remark, the sidings at Washwood Heath were a lot like life…there was an up side and a down side! The Up Side was made up of about 27 roads, some of which were the domain of the impressive and extraordinarily long Cartic trains. It was difficult to ignore these seemingly endless trains, which consisted of articulated sets of double decked car transporter wagons (4 wagons in each articulated set, but only 5 bogies per set). These transported saloon cars fresh off the assembly lines at Longbridge and Cowley (Austin Rover) to various holding areas around the country. I always used to keep an eye out for the single decked Comtic wagons, which transported the brand new Land Rovers…forever hoping that one might come adrift and roll off in my direction! However, we were located on the Down Side, which wasn't nearly as exciting. Apart from the RMC discharge road, which also incorporated a concrete sleeper loading gantry, there were just a couple of through sidings and about three CE roads.

Metro-Cammel

A trainman's other involvement within the confines of Washwood Heath was the occasional working to and from the Metro-Cammel factory (latterly GEC-Alsthom), situated next to the Down Side Sidings. Signing on at 0525, a driver and guard would be dispatched light engine to collect a rake of Mark IV coaches, which sometimes had a Class 82 DVT (Driving Van Trailer) tagged on the end. Entry into the factory was achieved by means of an electronic ground frame, similar to the one at Cliffe Hill. Once the train was ready to depart, it would be drawn straight out and run round. Trains arriving from the Down direction could be propelled in though, provided the guard kept a watchful eye on the road crossing. It was another one of those places where no one was ever seen using the access road, but on the rare occasion where a train had to propel in, there would suddenly be a build up of traffic! Whether delivering or collecting the rolling stock, the train would be routed via Nuneaton and the South Leicester Line, with relief usually scheduled at Leicester.

The RMC Discharge Point

Back at the hopper house, a couple of blasts on the horn would alert the RMC operative to our presence, who would then appear to open the control room and start the conveyor belt. Wagons had to be unloaded one at a time under instruction from the guard, so he would obtain a pair of two-way radios from the control room, handing one to the driver and keeping the other for himself. The engines would then be allowed to proceed through the hopper house and set the first wagon for unloading. On the underside of each wagon were three air operated doors and once these were positioned over the pit between the rails, an air line would be connected to the wagon and the doors opened. The stone would then drop into the pit and onto the conveyor belt below, to be deposited onto its corresponding pile in the adjacent storage yard. The train delivered different grades of limestone, starting with dust at one end of the scale, right up through 5, 10, 20mm, etc, to MOT (Type 1), but their positions in the train were dependent on the original train preparer at Peak Forest. Normally the different grades of stone were kept together in batches (e.g. four wagons of dust, six of 10mm, etc), but sometimes the odd wagon of MOT might pop up unexpectedly, which meant the RMC operative would have to dash into the control room and stop the conveyor belt, before re-setting the tripper to the correct pile.

From the guard's point of view, the radio commands were very simple: Forward, Stop (although most people shouted an enthusiastic Whoa!), and Set back. You hoped not to use the last command too often, as it meant the wagon had overshot! Unfortunately, one particular trainman was afflicted with a stutter, which became more pronounced under stressful conditions, so his commands for each wagon movement often went thus: "FFForward…SSt…SSt…oh sod it…Set back!" Whenever he was booked as the guard, most secondmen exchanged places with him, as it was the only way to get finished on time! It would have to be an act of pure desperation by the secondman though, as not many were willing to give up their comfortable position up front, in order to spend several hours setting wagons in an extremely dusty environment! During the winter months, it could be a bitterly cold environment too, so it was in the guard's best interest to set the wagons correctly first time, every time. Even so, it could take nearly three hours for the train to be unloaded, but a guard with a bit of experience could reduce this time slightly; The train could be sent forward as the previously emptied wagon was still having its last door closed. By the time the driver got the train under way, the air line could be removed and connected to the next wagon. As soon as its first door reached the pit, it could be opened whilst the train was still on the move. Providing the stone was flowing nicely and the driver kept a steady pace, the second and third doors could be opened also, resulting in most of the wagon being discharged before the train

82

had to be halted again. This was by no means a recommended method, but it could be an extremely efficient way of unloading the train, providing certain conditions were in the guard's favour…the first being that he was particularly quick on his toes! It also hinged on the wagons containing what the train list said they did, and the air line successfully popping off the wagons each time…more than once it got stretched a lot further than it was designed to do, as the guard struggled to pull it off the moving train! Once this level of skill had been achieved, the RMC operative usually left you to it, whilst he fired up his loading shovel and disappeared into the storage yard to keep his stone piles tidy.

Finally, and with always much relief, the last wagon would be set and the secondman asked to return the radio. After being discharged, the guard would ensure its doors had closed correctly and the air line removed before returning to the engine with the secondman. If the guard was on the ball, he would've already made out a driver's slip on the journey down, so all that remained would be to hand it to the driver. Permission would then be obtained from the signalman to proceed onto the Down Goods again, and once in position, the guard would uncouple the engines and remain with the train, whilst the driver and secondman continued to Saltley to run round. After the monotony of unloading wagons, running round essentially signified the end of the work and offered a welcome change of scenery. The area around Saltley was quite a hive of activity, with the depot and Landor Street Junction on one side and Lawley Street Freightliner Terminal and Saltley PSB on the other. Less than a mile away was Grand Junction, where three busy railway arteries joined just before New Street itself. As it was often dusk by the time the engines were run round, the illuminated skyline of Birmingham provided a stark contrast to the dull, but unmistakable gas holders of Washwood Heath. Before alighting, the guard would've taken a spare tail lamp with him to place on the end of the train, thus saving himself some unnecessary walking. Once the engines had trundled past on their return, there would be a further wait whilst the signalman routed them back onto the train at the other end and the secondman coupled up. Although the guard couldn't see any of this taking place, he would eventually hear the wagon brakes blowing off and observe the couplings stretching out slightly, at which point he would conduct a brake test. Assuming everything was in order, he could then finally return to his chosen cab and settle back for the return journey. As with most jobs, toilet facilities were few and far between, so in an effort to protect their modesty, most train crew would retire to the engine room. One trainman however, learnt never to perform the first call of nature through the radiator grille of a Class 37. Just as he was completing this very necessary task, the cooling fan kicked in, sucking the previous contents of his bladder back all over his trousers!

Once the bright lights of Birmingham and its industrial outskirts had receded, the return to Derby was generally dark and uneventful. The guard sensed the previous landmarks only in his periphery, from his position in the second engine. The brightly lit platforms of Water Orton, Wilnecote and Tamworth would flash past, along with the oil terminal at Kingsbury. The speed restriction at Burton would be registered as a hiss of air and a dull thump, as the driver cancelled the AWS in his cab up front. After the silent, brooding presence of Drakelow and Willington had been left behind, the guard might stick his head out the window at Peartree, just to ensure that the train was actually being routed into the station for relief, and not down the goods line. The latter option could involve some delay in being relieved and consequently signing off duty…which was a rather unwelcome development, particularly on a Friday night! After being relieved, the crew could finally return to 4 Shed with the satisfaction that another consignment of Derbyshire stone had been successfully delivered to Washwood Heath.

At this point in my life, I was still residing with my parents in Darley Abbey, which in very rough railway geographical terms, is situated between St. Mary's Goods Yard and Little Eaton Junction, (two places now consigned to the history books). Even though the old village is about a mile away from the tracks, train noises were still clearly audible...especially ones that involved two 37s! My Dad was familiar with our approximate time of arrival back in Derby, and whenever he heard the unmistakeable sound of the train powering north towards Duffield, he knew that within the next half hour, I'd be stepping through the front door!

As with most jobs after 1992...things changed! A single Class 60 replaced the familiar Class 37s, and for me, the mighty Washwood Heath began to lose its appeal slightly. Not that there was anything wrong with Class 60s. Once their initial mechanical problems had been solved, they eventually proved to be efficient, powerful engines, but being new they lacked character, charm and individuality compared with the 37s. I know there were many people who said the same thing when diesels replaced steam, and now here I am, saying it when diesels replace diesels!

A regular pair on the Washwood Heath were 37686 + 687, shown here receiving attention at Buxton before their next duty. The wagons themselves would be loaded at the RMC quarry at Dove Holes. Photo: P. Helme, circa 1988.

Epilogue

Although I was not aware of it at the time, looking back, I think the true railway life ended for me on the 5th of April 1992. On this normal, inconsequential day, the London Midland Region ceased to exist, and the job I knew and loved began to turn into something I barely recognised. From that point onwards, whether by accident or design, management made the job so unpalatable and unrewarding, that to my mind it practically amounted to constructive dismissal. I had done everything the railway asked of me, and more, but its new masters were not interested. I continued to fulfil my contract to them, but they were no longer willing or able to fulfil theirs. Subtle changes were initiated that eventually had devastating consequences. Things were taken from us and promises were broken…for me, it was the end of the line.

As the trend continued towards transporting more freight by road, I obtained a HGV1 licence and became a driver in the road haulage industry instead. The irony being that, at the time of writing, I am still transporting aggregates, and still waiting around in quarries and other associated loading facilities…in fact I am probably one of the few people who has transported aggregates to and from Chaddesden, Stud Farm and Bardon Hill, both by rail and road! But perhaps one day though, I might be reconciled with the railway in its next evolution…a bit further down the line? You can take the man from the railway, but you can't take the railway from the man.

The remaining freight engines at 4 Shed are lined up for a final photo call. Photo: C. Nutty, Apr 94.

Glossary

AWS	Automatic Warning System
BIS	Battery Isolation Switch
BREL	British Rail Engineering Limited
CE	Civil Engineers
DMU	Diesel Multiple Unit
DOO	Driver Only Operated
DSD	Driver's Safety Device
HST	High Speed Train
LRT	London Regional Transport
MGR	Merry Go Round
PSB	Power Signal Box
RMC	Ready Mixed Concrete
RTC	Railway Technical Centre
TCS	Train Crew Supervisor
TOPS	Total Operations Control System
TPO	Travelling Post Office